INDIA
Rich Agriculture: Poor Farmers (Income Policy for Farmers)

by

Dr. R.L. Pitale

2016

Daya Publishing House®

A Division of

Astral International Pvt. Ltd.

New Delhi - 110 002

First Published, 2007
Reprinted, 2016

ISBN: 978-81-7035-457-4 (Hardbound)

Published by : **Daya Publishing House®**
A Division of
Astral International Pvt. Ltd.
– ISO 9001:2008 Certified Company –
4760-61/23, Ansari Road, Darya Ganj
New Delhi-110 002
Ph. 011-43549197, 23278134
E-mail: info@astralint.com
Website: www.astralint.com

Laser Typesetting : **Classic Computer Services**
Delhi - 110 035

Printed at : **Chawla Offset Printer**

PRINTED IN INDIA

Acknowledgement

The genesis of writing this book and many thoughts contained in the book is the outcome of author's discussion and interaction with Prof. Dr. V M Vaidya, Head of Economics Dept. of Nagpur University who died recently. Author gratefully acknowledges his contribution. The discussions with Shri B Brahma and Shri R P Bhargava, Directors of the Commission for Agriculture Costs and Prices were very useful and I thank them for their assistance. For encouragement to write the book and to sustain the stamina, the assistance of my wife Mrs Neela, my sons, Ashish and Manish and my daughters-in-law Yogita and Purvesha is acknowledged with love. My three grand children Aastha, Parikshit and Nishtha kept me cheerful while writing the book for which they deserve all my affection.

Preface

Indian farmers are second to none in production and productivity inspite of the fact that millions are marginal and small farmers. The farmers took up the challenge to make India self sufficient in food grains and agriculture products. They adopted improved agriculture technology as efficiently as farmers in developed countries without much financial subsidies unlike their counterparts in developed countries. In spite of this record breaking performance economic condition of the farmers did not improve as much as it should have. A paradoxical situation has arisen wherein poor farmers are living in rich agriculture. During the last five years farmers have faced fall in their income. The ground level economic situation of farmers assessed by the National Sample Survey Organization (NSSO) in its 59TH Round (2005) has revealed that farming is becoming an un-popular occupation. The Survey has revealed that given the choice, about 40 per cent of the farmers said that they would quit farming and 27 per cent of the farmers said that they did not like farming because it is not profitable while 8 per cent felt that it is a risky occupation. The clear message is that farmers' income is going down and farmers consider that farming is no longer remunerative enough.

It means that increase in agriculture production and productivity has not adequately led to increase in farmer's income on a sustained basis. While all attention is concentrated on increase in agriculture production, the agriculture policy is not yet seriously oriented to enhance farmers' income. How to enhance farmers' income on sustained basis is the subject matter and theme of this book. Without getting bogged down with too much historical analysis of agriculture growth, the focus has been kept on how to increase farmers' income. The available information and data from government sources has been utilized to formulate strategies and programs for increasing farmers' income. As government took initiative in formulating Green Revolution Strategy to make India self sufficient in food grains, similarly government will have to focus attention on Income Revolution for farmers to ensure sustained increase in their income. In fact, farmers will have to be more active to ask for the implementation of strategy and programs suggested in the book. The NGOs and experts can play pro-active role in organizing the farmers to demand income due to them.

The beginning of civilization depended on agriculture, so does its future. But this is possible if farmers get grains and not the chaff only.

June, 2006 **Dr. R.L. Pitale**

Contents

List of Tables and Annexures

Annexures

Chapter 1

INDIA:
Rich Agriculture : Poor Farmers
(From Farm to Farmers)

Status of Indian Agriculture: Profile of Farms and Farmers

Small farmers of India competed well with the large farmers of developed countries in increasing the agricultural production and especially of food grains. They proved that if the requisite inputs and technologically improved crop varieties are provided they are capable of improving the performance of Indian agriculture. But there is limit to small scale operation. In the last five years, the Indian farmers are facing the income crisis.

It is interesting to observe that since 1950, the number of cultivators have gone up from 69.9 million to 127.3 million in 2001 indicating thereby, inter alia, the fragmentation of land due to pressure of population on land. Besides this, many cultivators with small land holdings seem to have sold of their land to meet their needs adding to number of agricultural labourers. Number of agriculture labourers increased from 27.3 million in 1950 to 106.8 million in 2001. The details may be seen in the Table 1.

Table 1: Structure of Agrarian Population

(million)

Year	*Total Population*	*Rural*	*Cultivators*	*Agri-Labour*	*Total (4+5)*
(1)	*(2)*	*(3)*	*(4)*	*(5)*	*(6)*
1951	361.1	298.6	**69.9**	**27.3**	97.2
		(82.7)	**(71.9)**	**(28.1)**	(100)
1971	548.2	439.0	78.2	47.5	125.7
		(80.1)	(62.2)	(37.8)	(100)
1991	846.4	628.9	110.7	74.6	185.3
		(74.3)	(59.7)	(40.3)	(100)
2001	1028.7	742.6	**127.3**	**106.8**	234.1
		(72.2)	**(54.4)**	**(45.6)**	(100)

Source: Agriculture Statistics at a Glance 2004. Ministry of Agriculture, Govt of India. Data In bracket show the percentage.

The Table 1 shows that proportion of cultivators in active agriculture population (cultivators plus agri-labourers) which was 71.9 per cent in 1950 decreased to 54.4 per cent in 2001 while proportion of agriculture labour increased from 28.1 per cent to 45.6 per cent during the same period. It indicates to a large extent the fragmentation of land due to pressure of population on agriculture land as reflected in increased number of cultivators from 69.9 million in 1950 to 127.3 million in 2001. The proportionate decrease in cultivators also shows some shift of this group to land less labours whose number increased from 27.3 million in 1951 to 106.8 million besides the increase in landless labour. The ratio of cultivators to agriculture labour which was 2.7 in 1951 has fallen down to 1.2. Thus comparatively there are less number of cultivators to support agriculture labour in 2001 compared to 1951.

Rich Agriculture

The current situation of the farm sector in India is one of rich agriculture but poor farmers. On the one hand small farmers have made India self sufficient in food grains but by the end of the 20th century the farmers have become poor. Their average per capita incomes in absolute and relative terms declined over the period. This is a serious issue for the economy as no progress will be worth the name if 72 per cent of India's population continues to face the grim situation of falling incomes. A brief profile of rich agriculture is summarized below:

Rich Agriculture

1. **Food grains:** 106.42 million tonnes 1970-71. 212.05 mt in 2003-04
Yield: 872 kg/hect.1970-71. 1704 kg/hect 2003-04
2. **Stock of Cereals** (Central and States): Highest at 58.11 million tonnes in 2002
3. **Buffer Stock of Cereals:** Central Pool: 24.41 mt in 2004-05 against stipulated 18.8 mt.
4. **Cropping Intensity:** 118.2 in 1970-71. 133.2 in 2000-01
5. **Area Sown more than once:** 25.52 million hectare 1970-71. 46.64 mh in 2000-01
6. **Gross area Irrigated:** 38.2 mh 1970-71. 75.14 mh 2000-01
7. Position in World Agriculture

Item	*Rank*	*Next to*
Irrigated Area	1st	
Wheat	2nd	China
Rice	2nd	China
Cereals	3rd	China, USA
Pulses	1st	
Oil Seeds	2nd	China
Fruits	2nd	China
Sugarcane	2nd	Brazil
Tea	1st	
Jute	1st	
Cotton	4th	China, USA, Pakistan
Tobacco	2nd	China
Milk	1st	
Coffee	6th	Brazil, Vietnam, Columbia, Indonesia, Mexico

8. Food grains exports higher than imports
9. Potential to increase production to 400 million tonnes in the next five to ten years

Source: Agricultural Statistics at A Glance 2004 Ministry of Agriculture, Govt. of India.

From the above Box it will be clear that agriculture sector in terms of production and productivity has become quite rich. India has become self sufficient in agri-produce and can compete with rest of the world if developed countries reduce their subsidies to farmers. The area under irrigation has gone up during the last 30 years significantly and there is great potential to be tapped. Crop intensity is a singular factor that has offset the disadvantage of small size of the farms. Production structure is quite diversified. In terms of production it ranks first and second in the world for number of commodities. The cost of production continues to be low and farm labour contributes much for the increase in production. Though productivity is nearly half the productivity by world standards there is great potential to tap it by increasing the intensity of production. It is also to be understood that indiscriminate use of fertilizers and other chemicals may increase the productivity but there is danger of contaminating the produce with the chemical substances. The developed countries have realized the perils of this increased chemical productivity and are now going in for more of organic production even if the productivity comes down.

Poor Farmers

In spite of such rich agriculture sector the gains to the farmers have not been commensurate and especially since the beginning of 21st century. Farmer finds himself economically poor and most of the gains of rich agriculture have been appropriated by other sections of the community. Not much attention has been paid to the income that accrues to farmers and especially marginal farmers. With the increased production, the surpluses in agriculture produce have arisen resulting in fall in prices. The regulated agri-markets have increased his cost of marketing. Under the liberalized free trade regime under WTO he is exposed to market forces which are detrimental to his welfare. The reduction in input subsidies have resulted in increased operational cost of production. The farmer has been caught in treacherous situation of rising cost of production and falling prices for his produce. It is travesty of facts that rich agriculture has led to more poor farmers rather than making them rich. The income and fiscal policies of the government have widened the gap between the farmers and others in absolute and relative terms. No economic indicators have been constructed to measure the income of the farmers/rural people and others and no monitoring mechanism to divert the income to farmers. The following Box gives the indicators of poor farmers.

There is virtually no monitoring of increase in farmers' income on the pattern of schemes and programs for increasing produce. The fall out effect of increased production and productivity in agriculture has not been particularly positive for marginal and small farmers as also for agriculture labour as revealed from the following Box. This is mainly due to the fact that the proportionate share of agri-GDP in total GDP has decreased but the burden of rural population on the farmers continues to be the same or increasing. The volume of absolute increase in Agri-GDP falls much short of population pressure due to lack of agro-related activities. There is only one way passage of production from rural areas to urban areas but there is not much of return flow of incomes to farmers. The agro-processing activities are not available to farmers and movements of agri-produce to urban regulated markets are not friendly. With surplus production of agri-produce vis-à-vis current demand the result is fall in prices which further affect his income adversely as can be seen during the last five years. Farmer is caught in increased yields, surplus and low prices.

Poor Farmers

A. Macro-Indicators

1. Fall in Average per capita Agri-GDP (Ratio of Agri-GDP to Rural Population)

   1990-91: Rs. 3802 (Rs.318/–per month)

   2002-03: Rs. 3732 (Rs. 311/–pm)

   Absolute fall in per capita rural income by Rs.72/–over 12 years period.
2. **Rural-Urban Real Income Differential:** Average rural real income of Rs. 3732 is lower by 10 times the Urban average real per capita GDP of Rs. 34,660.
3. **Fall in share of Agri-GDP:** 1993-94: 31 per cent 2003-04: 22 per cent. Comparatively lower volume of income generated in Agri-Sector with high proportion of rural population. Average per capita Agri-GDP lowest in Bihar: Rs.1503/-(Rs.125.3 per month) and highest in Punjab at Rs. 10,284 (Rs. 857 pm). Bihar rural/farmers income is one third of national average. Extremely poor farmers.
4. **Terms of Trade (1990-91) Static**: Ratio of index of prices received by agri-sector and prices paid to non-agri sectors: 1994-95: 106.2, 2000-01: 102.8, 2002-03: 106.8. Over a period of ten years TT is virtually static and decreased in 2002-03 showing adverse impact on farmers' income.

B. Micro-Indicators

1. **Low Monthly Per Capita Expenditure (MPCE) of Farmer Households: 2003:** NSSO 59th Round: Rs. 502.83. Lower by 9.3 per cent compared to all rural HHs. Lowest in Orissa Rs. 341.75; close to poverty line expenditure of Rs. 327.56 pm estimated by the Planning Commission.
2. **Low and Falling Income of Farmers: Farming Unpopular Occupation:** NSSO 59th Round (2003): 40 per cent prefer to quit farming, 27 per cent consider farming un-profitable, 9 per cent – risky proposition.
3. **Indebtedness of Farmers (NSSO 59th Round 2003):** Out of 89.35 million farmers 43.42 million indebted. 1 acre or less land HH accounted for 66 per cent of all farmers. 36 per cent loans from banks and 26 per cent money lenders.
4. Falling prices of Agri-produce (WPI 1993-94=100): per cent Variation

   Food grains: 2002-03: 3.3 per cent; 2003-04: –0.1

   Sugar: 2002-03: 5.9 per cent; 2003-04: 0.1
5. **MSP covers only Cost of Production:** No profit/return to farmer over his cost of cultivation. Family labour and rent of the land account about 1/3rd to ½ of cost of cultivation. Imputed value of labour in the cost of production is surviving limit of farmer.
6. **Market Prices fall below MSP:** No assured intervention purchases by procurement agencies especially in North-East States for wheat. This has been experienced for other commodities. Open market auction price of onions fell to lowest level at Rs.10/–per quintal in 2004-05 in Nasik Market of Maharashtra.
7. Decrease in Real MSP
8. Static Agri-labour Real Wages during the last three years in most of the States.

While the agriculture production over the period increased almost four times during the period, the proportionate balance between cultivators and agri-labour virtually reversed between 1951 to 2001. The production of food grains and other commercial crops except oilseeds compared to the current domestic demand being higher, has resulted in fall in prices or remained static as seen in the whole sale price index of agriculture commodities during the last 5 years. This has led to less income to farmers. The average size of farm also decreased from 1.57 to 1.41 hectares indicating further uneconomic size of land.

The separate figures of average per capita income of rural population is not available or published. But the GDP of agriculture sector and population in the rural sector can give a reasonable and reliable figure of per capita GDP in agriculture sector. The comparative figures of Agri-sector GDP (excluding value of income from livestock) and rural population in 1991-92 and 2002-03 shows that the per capita GDP in real terms (93-94 prices) of farm sector was Rs. 3802 (Rs. 318/– per capita per month) in 1991-92 compared to Rs. 3,732 (Rs. 311/– per capita per month). This shows that over the 12 year period since 1991-92, the per capita GDP of farm sector population on a point to point basis decreased in absolute terms by Rs. 70. In the absence of separate estimates for income profile of the farmers the average per capita GDP of the farm sector is good bench mark to start with. The poverty line in 1999-2000 at all India level as estimated by the Planning Commission is Rs. 327.56 per month (Rs. 3936/– per annum). This is the grim situation of farm sector population and there is no wonder that farmers are committing suicides.

The information given in the above Box shows that number of economic indicators point out clearly that production, prices and markets have not been favourable to farmers. This has resulted in falling incomes and making farmers poor. Increased production and productivity in the farm sector is no guarantee that farmers economic status is improving. The gains of increased production and productivity have to pass to farmers in higher incomes. This does not seem to have happened by the turn of the century. Alternatively, it is evident that market for agriculture and current scheme of regulated markets have increased the cost of the marketing for the farmers. In the supply chain farmer has become a weak link. The recent Studies of the Federation of Indian Chambers and Commerce and Industry (FICCI) and the Asian Development Bank (ADB) illustrate this aspect.

The loss to the farmer under the existing Agriculture Produce and Marketing Act (APMA) due to mark-up at different stages of marketing is shown in the following Table.

Table 2: APMA: Adding Cost and No Value

Margin from Farmers to Wholesaler: 30-35 per cent
Wastage: 15-25 per cent
Transportation: 10 per cent
Total mark-up in marketing chain 60 to 75 per cent

Source: FICCI: 75th Platinum Jubilee Series-2002.

The table clearly shows that with reform of APMA farmers' losses can be reduced in transportation and wastage by 25-30 per cent. Alternative measure of increase in income is the difference in the farm-gate price to the produce of the farmer and subsequent stages of marketing which is shown in the following Table.

Table 3: Supply Chain of Select Agricultural Commodities

Rice	Wheat	Apple	Onion	Groundnut
Producer				
100	100	100	100	100
Miller	Primary Wholesaler	Forwarding Agent	Local Commission	Merchant Agent
129	119	128	174	103
Wholesaler	Secondary Wholesaler	Commission Agent	Wholesaler	Oil Miller
142	139	169	182	135
Retailer	Retailer	Wholesaler	Retailer	Wholesaler
154	150	187	232	144

Source: ADB Report: May 2004/ TA 4192-ind

The above Table shows the price jack up of farm produce from "Farm Gate" to the "Retailer" and finally much more to the "Lunch Table" (consumer). If the farmer is linked, with reform in APMA, to wholesaler directly, he is likely to get increase in income by about 25-30 per cent. But that needs change in APMA of the State governments, which is not forthcoming.

The above Tables show the extent to which the farmers have to pay the higher marketing cost and how much less the farmer gets in a supply chain. The main gainers of agri-produce and farmers' productivity are the whole sellers and retailers and processors of agri-produce.

The main problem in the agriculture sector is not so much lack of production and productivity but assured and sustained increase in farmers' income. The present marketing system is not farmer friendly, government support and intervention to provide remunerative prices is dwindling and overall government investment in capital formation in agriculture has not been sufficient to generate economic activities in rural sector as was done vigorously during

Green Revolution in 1970s and early 1980s. These macro level factors can be energized in favour of the farmers but there are certain inherent constraints of the agriculture sector of the economy that will need a new look and policy to introduce changes to correct these constraints.

In the first phase of Green Revolution, constraints of small size of farms was managed by providing package of inputs and incentives to increase production. In scarcity phase of agri-produce, farmers got better return for their produce from small farms. Till end of 1980s, farm sector was protected through effective government intervention, input subsidies and protection from imports of agri-produce. Since 1990-91 with the liberalization of economic policies, WTO Membership from 1995 and agri-produce surpluses arising in the farm sector coupled with less than adequate intervention by the government, small farmers in particular found it difficult to compete in the market. The economic limitation of small operation has surfaced as a critical factor to get adequate and sustained increase in income. That calls for structural, organizational and institutional changes in managing the farm sector in India. What India needs now is the Incomes Policy for Farmers. Agriculture Policy oriented towards production and productivity alone is not going to provide sustained increase in income to farmers. Hence, new framework for sustained increase in income is to be evolved.

The situation of falling income of farmers arose in European Union where in production increased but incomes of the farmers started lagging behind in 1970s. They changed the slant of agriculture policy to ensure increase in income and provide fair standard of living for farmers. Common Agriculture Policy (CAP) of EU, inter alia, designed incomes policy for EU farmers to shift emphasis from agriculture to incomes of the farmers by reorganizing the rural sector through better domestic price support, reducing number of people employed in agriculture and promoting the formation of larger and more efficient units of agriculture production. China has off late realized that farmers' earnings increased a year-on-year 5.4 per cent in the first four years of reform period but incomes shrank annually in the past five years. China's Minister for Agriculture has recently announced that farmers' income is to be increased in the next five years. Thus it is the farmers' income that is in the forefront of economic policy and not the agriculture production alone.

Though no separate Per Capita GDP for agriculture sector is calculated at the national level and published, it can be calculated at the All India and State level by taking into account the GDP from agriculture and the rural population as broad bench mark levels. The State-wise per capita Agri-GDP can be a good indicator of the level of income of the rural people as also of farmers who contribute mainly to agri-GDP. The State-wise per capita agri-GDP for 1990-91 and 2001-02 has been arrived at on the basis of total real value of output (1993-94 prices) from agriculture and livestock and rural populations of the respective years (Annexure I). The following Table shows in descending order of per capita agri-GDP for States for 2001-02. This shows level and extent of differences amongst the States.

Table 4: State-wise Per Capita Agri-GDP* 2001-02 (1993-94 prices) Rs.

Sl.No.	State	Per Capita Agri-GDP	Share of Agri-GDP In Total State GDP(%)	% Rural Population
1.	Punjab	12,337	38.7	65.8
2.	Haryana	9,374	30.8	70.8
3.	Karnataka	6,676	24.2	65.9
4.	Goa	6,582	6.6	
5.	Mizoram	6,244	N.A.	—
6.	Nagaland	5,987	N.A.	—
7.	Maharashtra	5,712	13.9	58.6
8.	Gujarat	5,539	15.6	62.5
9.	Tamilnadu	5,135	15.2	55.8
10.	J & K	5,005	27.3	90.2
11.	Andhra Pradesh	4,986	24.2	72.5
12.	Tripura	4,721	18.2	—
13.	Kerala	4,417	18.9	74.0
14.	West Bengal	4,507	22.6	72.0
15.	Madhya Pradesh	4,421	26.6	73.4
16.	Himachal Pradesh	4,258	17.1	90.2
17.	Arunachal Pradesh	3,842**	20.2	—

Contd..

Table 4–Contd...

Sl.No.	State	Per Capita Agri-GDP	Share of Agri-GDP In Total State GDP(%)	% Rural Population
18.	Rajasthan	3,652**	28.1	76.5
19.	Uttar Pradesh	3,571	33.2	79.2
20.	Meghalaya	3,408	21.6	—
21.	Sikkim	3,377**	N.A.	88.8
22.	Orissa	3,104**	25.4	84.8
23.	Assam	3,084	28.9	87.3
24.	Manipur	3,025**	20.9	—
25.	Bihar	2,317**	35.2	89.4

* Value of GDP from Agriculture and Livestock

** Per Capita Agri-GDP is lower in 2001-02 compared to 1990-91 on point to point basis.

The per capita Agri-GDP crucially depends on the size of the total Agri-GDP of the State. The rural population, inspite of migration to urban areas, is increasing. Family welfare measures has limited impact on reducing the rural population. Hence, it is the accelerated increase in the size of Agri-GDP alone that can increase income of the farmers in particular and rural people in general. In developed countries where size of the population is static, rural population could be transferred to urban areas in industrial and services sector. Hence their rural population is around 5 per cent of total population and contribution of Agri-GDP to total GDP is around 3 per cent. Such a model can not be emulated in India. The declining proportion of Agri-GDP in total GDP is not a happy situation and is a matter of concern. Unless this is realized attention will not be focussed on this crucial limitation. India has a very big agriculture sector with millions of farmers whose lot can not be improved if the size of the Agri-GDP is shrinking and its proportionate share in GDP is falling.

The rural sector/areas are like agro based nations with limited backward and forward linkages to developed urban areas. The income generation in rural areas, except in States like Punjab and Haryana, by rural and farmer population is scanty and not much could be developed on the side of non-farm activities. Hence entire burden is to fall on the farms and borne by the farmers. With small size of farms, economic viability can not be stretched beyond a limit. Hence, the low per capita Agri-GDP is the resultant effect inspite of the fact these very small farmers increased agriculture production and productivity and made India self sufficient in food grains. Farmers gave food security but in turn did not get income security for themselves. Therefore, in all future policies and programs, farmer's income is to be at the centre stage of development.

The Indian farmers residing in 6.38 lakh villages producing 22 per cent of GDP have to carry burden of 741.66 million people under these economic conditions. The income level in the farm sector is then the function of volume of agri-GDP produced, size of the agriculture and total rural population and the return that he gets for his produce and the flow of resources, if any, from urban to rural areas.

The developed countries may take small share of Agri-GDP in total GDP as an indicator of rapid development and less dependence on agriculture but it can not be measure of economic development for India whose 72 per cent of population resides in rural areas. India requires high volume of Agri-GDP to sustain and increase the standard of living in rural areas because India can not afford to de-populate its rural population. It will be interesting to know that total population of 15 European Union countries is 375.3 million which comes to only less than half the rural population India at 742.6 million. All the 20 countries of EU and 18 countries of Eastern Europe put together have a population of 581.8 million which is still less than the rural population of India. With stable population or declining population in Europe it can be feasible for them to de-populate their rural areas and provide jobs and income in urban industrial areas but this model can not work for India whose large and growing population resides in rural areas.

For just 2 per cent of rural population EU spends under various subsidy and direct payments $300 billion *i.e.* about Rs.13.5 lakh cro. which is about 55 per cent of India's real GDP. This is the magnitude of flow of resources to EU's tiny farm sector. India can ill afford such cash and kind support to farmers. The answer lies in generating incomes by locating and shifting agro-based and other related economic activities at the farm gates of cluster of villages. The circular flow of income to rural areas through public-private partnership needs a big boost and price support to farmers has to be sustained so that their incomes do not fall. Unless this mechanism is placed on a sound footing farmers will be in misery and no amount of increase in productivity is going to provide any relief to farmers. The chemical input based increase in production and productivity of the farmer in the Green Revolution is not a guarantee that farmers' income will increase. Specific strategies and policy and programs focussing on farmer's income is required to be implemented without any delay. In the 1970s the focus was shifted from "land economics" to "production economics" and self sufficiency in food grains was achieved in a short period of time. Now the focus has to be "farmers' income" that is to be increased on a sustained basis in certain time frame.

The physical dimension of India's rural sector is unique and highly complicated. The average population per village at the all India level as per 2001 population Census is 1,181 people and 80 per cent farmers are marginal and small farmers. This situation is more or less true for most of the States. It is in tiny villages and cluster of such villages that jobs are to be created primarily on farms and agro-based activities on a sustainable basis. If the Agri-GDP falls proportionately to total GDP and increases at a snails pace of 1.5 per cent or sometimes negative as has been witnessed during the last three years, how can the employment and income of the farmers in particular and rural people in general can be raised.

If farmers' income level is to be raised what is required is to have higher levels of Agri-GDP and agro-based activities and better return for the agri-produce of the farmers and reducing his marketing cost. This three pronged attack can alone increase the income levels of farmers and not merely increase in production and productivity. To bring about this change farmers have to unite themselves under the banner of commodity that they produce. Commodity Boards for different agri-produce set up and managed by the farmers themselves as is being done by the farmers in developed countries will be permanent institutional mechanism that will safeguard their incomes in future. The palliatives of government programs and weak crop insurance and other schemes is hardly an answer for eradicating farmers' economic misery.

Small Farmer's Income

Before incomes policy for farmers is designed it is essential to understand the current nature and status of the farm sector. Some factors are directly related to farmers themselves and some fall in the area of government policy and programs. Basic to the farmer is the size of the farm *i.e.* his production unit. As detailed earlier, 80 per cent of the farmers are marginal and small farmers (up to 2 hectares) who cultivate 36 per cent of the area. Not only the size of the farm is small but they are scattered over large area. Hence their consolidation to make the farms big is not only difficult but seems impossible. The small piece of land is so dear to farmer that he does not want to part with its ownership. Livelihood of majority of farmers (marginal and small) is small piece of land.

Income of marginal and small farmers depends upon the yield from his small size of the land and the price he gets for his produce. Though the average yield of the farms has increased over the period, due to constraint of small size there is limit to increase production. As an illustration, income of the rice and wheat growing farmer can be assessed. In 2003-04 the average yield of paddy was 2051 kg per hectare and for wheat 2707 kg. per hectare. For a marginal farmer, assuming that his yield equals the average, then at minimum support price (MSP) of Rs. 550 per quintal for 2003-04, his income comes to Rs. 11,288 per hectare which means Rs. 940 per month. Taking family size of 4 persons, per capita income per month works out to 235. For two acre farmer it will be Rs. 470 per capita per month. In case of marginal wheat farmer it is Rs. 355 per capita per month.

This income would be further less if the size is less than one acre or yield low or the market price is below the MSP. The income base of the marginal and small farmer is slender *i.e.* if the yield or production goes down below the average or he does not get the MSP or market price is below MSP, he becomes financially critical or goes bankrupt. He has no margin left to repay the debt. Therefore, in the recent past when due to draught or flood or due to surplus production, either his production (yield) fell or market prices did not fetch enough income to him, marginal and small farmers' income decreased sharply leading to bankruptcy.

It is thus clear that with slender land base of the marginal and small farmers, slight variation in production level or MSP or market prices falling below MSP due to surplus of the agri-produce, farmer's income is significantly affected badly. Increase in farmers' income is greatly constrained by the size of the farm and insecurity in getting the remunerative price either MSP or open market price. Even the

MSP does not provide for return on managerial input of the farmers like any other business activity. MSP provides for the actual costs incurred including imputed rental value of owned land and family labour. His margin to survive is his own family labour and notional value of rent of his land.

One of the Millennium Studies of the Ministry of Agriculture and Cooperation, Government of India, titled "Cost of Cultivation and Farm Income" by Dr Abhijit Sen bears out the above income status of the farmers. The Study states "Farm size and cropping intensity show that average farm size has declined as a result of faster farm population than area cropped. Outcomes were less favourable in per cultivator terms than per hectare. Real farm business income per cultivator may have actually declined during 1990s. Farm incomes are insufficient for most small and marginal farmers.— Increase in output prices required to neutralize subsidy reduction are not large and the income implications of these can depress farmer's welfare significantly."

Farmers' Limitations

As detailed above the major limitation to earn higher and increasing income is the very small size of the land which he cultivates. Another factor is the very small size of the rural economy at the disaggregated level. Large number of villages have a population of 500 and below. Average size of the village ranges from 2000 to 5000 people. In that case there are hardly any off farming avenues to add to his income. In that case the entire economy is at subsistence level. With very little infrastructure of irrigation, roads, electricity etc the overall economic activity is very low. The financial institutions serving such areas neither have much business nor they can generate much activity in such areas. Marginal and small farmers' income virtually remains stagnant for years.

With very low or virtually no marketable surplus generated by marginal and small farmers the money income of these farmers continues to be low. The million dollar question is how to increase size of his land or how to increase operational efficiency of his farm by adding infrastructure assets such as irrigation and his ability to market his produce at remunerative price. The present marketing mechanism under Agriculture Produce Marketing Act (APMA) is neither cost saving nor providing better prices for his produce. The

MSP only provides for actual costs of production without providing for his managerial service.

The main issue is very low or poverty level income of marginal and small farmers numbering 92.82 million (80 per cent) cultivating 58.8 million hectare (36 per cent) of land. How to raise their income year after year on a sustained basis is the main problem of the Indian economy.

When the land size is sub-optimal and there is limit to enhance it with addition of infrastructure what kind of organizational and institutional changes would be required to make marginal and small farmers economically and financially well off is the main policy issue. Another difficulty is how to reduce pressure of population by shifting it from rural areas to urban areas. Unlike the developed countries, it is financially unmanageable to make direct income payments to farmers or subsidize them due to sheer large number. In developed countries of the OECD, Producer Support Estimate (PSE) which indicates the annual monetary value of gross transfers from consumers and taxpayers to agricultural producers account for 31 per cent of gross farm receipt in OECD. In case of Japan, PSE is 59 per cent, EU 35 per cent and USA 21 per cent. Farmers constitute about 3/5 per cent of total population in these countries. Due to sheer colossal financial resources required to give direct increase in income to Indian farmers, this route also can not be workable in India. Now developed countries are also under pressure under WTO to reduce income subsidies given to the farmers.

What then can be income raising opportunities for the marginal and small farmers ? Before this issue is considered it will be useful to understand the geography of farms and farmers to identify the farmer specific income generation avenues.

Limitations and New Initiatives

In formulating any strategy and policy for the farmers there are inherent structural and demographic limitations due to the existing conditions obtaining in rural sector in general and agriculture sector in particular. The structural limitation is very small size of land and large number of farmers. With the strong historical attachment to farm land and its ownership it is virtually difficult to increase of the farm size directly by expecting the farmers to surrender their land. It is only through intensity of cultivation through irrigation and high yielding varieties that the size of land can be increased implicitly. Another limitation is subsistence agriculture of large number of farmers especially of food grains and very little marketable surplus that they generate. Their holding capacity is very weak and hence in the post harvest period due to increased supplies they get lower prices for their produce. The marketing cost under the APMA reduce return on their sales and in surplus production situation, the open market prices fall below the MSP/SMP. Intervention purchases of public agencies except for rice and wheat in Punjab, Haryana and UP are far from satisfactory and not very helpful for farmers. On the demographic front, the rural population can not be de-populated by any incentive and the present voluntary migration from rural to urban areas is unbearable and threatening the break down of civic services in urban areas. In addition, agriculture is a State subject and the role of Central government is more of advisory and supporting nature. Much is to be done by the State governments. The increase in employment and income generation has to come largely from State policy for farmers.

In spite of these limitations, it is the strategy and the policies of the Central government that give the boost to agriculture sector as was done in the phase of the Green Revolution. In the next phase, it is the income of the farmers that has to be at the centre stage. It is the Income Revolution Policy that Central government will have to evolve in co-operation with State governments with initiatives on marketing agr-produce, institutionalising the Commodity Boards managed by the farmers and finally by activating the agro-processing at the farm gates that will help increase the volume of agri-GDP commensurate with the burden of rural population in each State. Before such a policy is spelt out it will be useful to understand the geography of farm sector and farmers.

Chapter 2

Geography of Farm Sector and Farmers

India with its vast gross cropped area of 187.9 million hectare covered in 14 agro-climatic zones has led to different crop intensities across different States. At the macro level with growing industrialization and development of services sectors share of agriculture in GDP (1993-94 prices) has come down to 22 per cent in 2002-03 compared to 31 per cent in 1993-94. However, Agri-GDP in absolute terms increased from Rs 2,41,967 cro. in 1993-94 to Rs. 3,15,635 cro. in 2003-04 *i.e.* increase of 30 per cent over a decade. India continues to be agricultural economy as 72 per cent of its population lives in rural area and primarily depends on agriculture for its livelihood. While the share of agri-GDP has declined, burden of population is the same which has led to declining per capita GDP of rural population. Added to that is the problem of small size of farms. 80 per cent of operational holdings are marginal and small.

The State-wise Agri-GDP shows that U.P., Maharashtra, A.P. and W.B contribute one third Agri-GDP to total Agri-GDP in 2001-02. Of the 25 States, 10 States contribute two third of total Agri-GDP. This can be seen in the Table 5.

The agricultural intensity is better measured by percentage share of Agri-GDP in total GDP of the State and not by the absolute amount. Punjab is more agri-intensive (38.7 per cent), followed by UP and Haryana in the North and A.P., Karnataka, M.P. and WB. in

South, Central and East respectively. These agri-intensive States contribute 68 per cent to total All India Agri-GDP. India's agri-sector performance depends on the production in these agri-intensive States.

Table 5: State Agri-GDP 2001-02

Rs. Crore

State	*Agri-GDP*	*% Share of Agri-GDP in State total GDP*
U.P.	38117	33.2
Maharashtra	23087	13.9
A.P.	21512	24.2
W.B.	20830	22.6
Karnataka	17234	24.4
Punjab	16454	38.7
Rajasthan	16107	28.1
Tamilnadu	14173	15.8
M.P.	14151	26.6
Gujarat	13063	15.6
Haryana	10736	30.8
Total	1,91,313	—
Total All India	2,79,871	20.2

Source: Agricultural Statistics At A Glance 2004. Ministry of Agriculture

Crop Intensity

Based on the agro-climatic conditions there is virtually geo-specialization of crops across the country. Three or four States produce around 50 per cent or more of total production of a commodity. This will be clear from the Table 6.

This intensity of crops shows the dependence of large number of farmers on such crops in those areas. Any adverse climatic condition for the crop or supply exceeding the demand leading to fall in prices affects the farmers adversely and particularly marginal and small farmers. From the point of view of policy making for crops and farmers, geographical distribution of farmers crop-wise assumes great importance.

Table 6: Three Largest Producing States of Major Crops 2002-03

Crop	*Cumulative Share of Production (per cent)*
Wheat	72.17 (U.P, Punjab, Haryana)
Rice	43.19 (W.B., Punjab, U.P.)
Coarse Cereals (Total)	46.25 (Maharashtra, Rajasthan, Karnataka)
Pulses	56.73 (MP., UP., Maharashtra)
Food grains (Total)	43.23 (U.P., Punjab, West Bengal)
Oilseeds	47.10 (M.P., Maharashtra, Rajasthan)
Sugarcane	66.00 (U.P., Maharashtra, Karnataka)
Cotton	61.58 (Maharashtra, Gujarat, A.P.)
Potato	79.90 (U.P., W.B., Bihar)
Onion	56.70 (Maharashtra, Gujarat, Karnataka)

Source: Agricultural Statistics At A Glance 2004. Ministry of Agriculture

Crop-wise Geographical Distribution of Farmers

The dimension of the problems faced by the farmers of a particular crop is revealed by the number of farmers cultivating that crop. The information of crop-wise number of farmers also helps in formulating policy and programs for those farmers. It also gives information on the area of cultivation of such crops. Crop-wise details of farmers and area cultivated by such farmers is given in the Table 7.

Table 7: Number of Farmers by Major Crops (Agriculture Census 1995-96)

Sl.No.	*Crop*	*No. of Holdings ('000)*	*Area ('000 hectare)*
1.	Paddy	**55,716**	45,824
2.	Wheat	**30,417**	25,163
	1+2	**86,133 (48.3)**	70.987 (49.3)
3.	Coarse Cereals Jowar, Bajara, Maize and Ragi)	**35,540 (19.9)**	31.045 (21.6)
4.	Pulses	**15,178 (8.5)**	9,184 (6.4)
5.	Oilseeds	20,264 (12.2)	17,275 (12.0)
6.	Sugarcane	6,592 (3.9)	3,926 (2.7)

Contd...

Table 7–Contd...

Sl.No.	*Crop*	*No. of Holdings ('000)*	*Area ('000 hectare)*
7.	Cotton	6,781 (4.0)	9.467 (6.6)
8.	Jute & Mesta	490	139
9.	Potato	4,768 (2.9)	1,138 (0.79)
10.	Chillies	2,508 (1.5)	737
	Total	**178,254**	**143,896**

Figures in bracket show percentage to total. Number of holdings is taken as number of farmers. Commodity-wise figure of farmers is higher than the number of holdings because the farmers are taking more than one crop during the year.

The above table shows that of the total number of farmers, 86.19 million farmers are rice and wheat farmers. They cultivate almost 50 per cent of agricultural land. 77 per cent of total farmers *i.e.*136.85 million farmers are food grains farmers (Rice, wheat, coarse cereals and pulses). Such is the heavy dependence of farmers on food grains production.

Therefore, the incomes of these farmers will depend upon the prices which they will receive from these crops and supply demand management by the government and conditions in the market. The food grains production compared to demand in the open market can lead to very significant fall in prices but for the price support provided by procurement arrangement by Food Corporation of India (FCI). Wherever such a support is lacking, the farmers suffer. Such a situation is being faced in North-East and West Bengal and also in case of coarse grains where FCI and NAFED procurement respectively is minimal or virtually non-existent. In these areas, market prices fell below the MSP and farmers faced low income crisis.

In the recent past, the sugarcane and cotton farmers (13.2 million) also suffered due to apparent surplus production leading to arrears of payment or low prices paid to farmers. The income situation of the marginal and small farmers will be further precarious.

Crop-wise Distribution of Marginal and Small Farmers

Due to small size of the farms, marginal and small food grains farmers are further vulnerable to market forces and due to inherent limitation of small quantity of production and transportation problems, government support mechanism also does not become much effective for them. The dimension of this group of farmers can be seen in the Table 8.

Table 8: Marginal and Small Farmers by Crops (Agriculture Census 1995-96)

Crop	*No. of Holdings ('000)*		*Area ('000 hectare)*	
	Marginal	*Small*	*Marginal*	*Small*
Paddy	36193	10052	13151	10471
Wheat	17572	5626	5685	4359
Jowar	3969	3365	1353	2617
Bajra	2591	1872	1005	1579
Arhar	2548	2267	453	686
Gram	2217	1581	576	846
Sugarcane	3112	1621	882	934
Cotton	1548	1947	726	1818
Groundnut	2618	1812	892	1517
Rapeseed	2599	1560	640	786

Above Table shows that marginal and small farmers constitute major proportions for Paddy and Wheat crops. In case of Wheat, 76 per cent of total Wheat growing farmers are marginal and small farmers cultivating 46.7 per cent of the area under Wheat. For Paddy, 83 per cent of Paddy growing farmers are marginal and small farmers and cultivate 51.5 per cent of area under Paddy. This is the situation more or less true in respect of other crops. Due to small scale operation these farmers are vulnerable to any adverse climatic conditions or fall in prices. In the first phase of Green Revolution marginal and small farmers with the support of irrigation, high yielding varieties and better prices due to scarcity of agri-produce got better returns. But off late during the last five years with enough supplies and better transport and supply management of food grains the prices started declining or remained static pushing down their income. Due to small size of the farm, diminishing returns seems to have commenced. The smallness of the farm could not be substituted by more irrigation or fertilizer or new varieties beyond a certain limit.

Increase in farm size and efficient scale of operation seems to be the solution to improve income situation of the farmer. The States having large proportion of marginal and small farmers have suffered most as seen in the number of persons below poverty line.

Small Farms, Small Farmers and Poverty

Out of 92.1 million marginal and small farmers 32 million *i.e.* almost one third are concentrated in U.P. and Bihar States. Of the total number of 21.25 million farmers of U.P, 19.3 million (91 per cent) are marginal and small farmers. Such is the grave situation with the fragmentation of land. In Bihar out of total 14.15 million farmers 12.8 million (90.7 per cent) are marginal and small farmers. Even in State like W.B. where land reforms is considered to have made a big stride, marginal and small farmers are 5 million (76.3 per cent) out of total 6.55 million farmers. Only in Punjab number of marginal and small farmers are 3.8 lakh (32.8 per cent) out of 1.09 million farmers. The average holdings size of marginal farmers is 0.4 hectare (about an acre) and of small farmers it is 1.42 hectare (about two and half acre). Average size of the holding comprising of all farmers was 1.57 hectare in 1991-92 which decreased to 1.41 hectare in 1995-96 as per the Agriculture Census.

In rural areas where the burden of population is high and ever increasing and in case of States where the proportion of marginal and small farmers is very high, the number and proportion of people below poverty line is also very high. With reference to above paragraph, percentage of persons below poverty line in rural areas in Orissa is highest at 48 per cent followed by Bihar 44.3 per cent, M.P 37 per cent and U.P and W.B. 30 per cent each. The lowest is Punjab at 6.35 per cent and Haryana at 8.27 per cent. There seems to be direct positive relationship between small size of the farm and the poverty in rural areas.

The 59th Round of NSSO in its Report on Income, Expenditure and Productive Assets {Report No.497 (59/33/5)} covering period from July 2002 to June 2003 and released in December 2005 shows that 60 per cent of rural households are farmer house holds. It is highest in J&K at 91 per cent followed by Chhatisgarh, Uttar Pradesh and Rajasthan at 76-77 per cent. The main source of income of the farmers is cultivation followed by wages. As per Survey, the average monthly income per farmer house hold from cultivation is Rs.969

and from wages Rs. 819, non-farm business Rs. 236 and animals Rs. 91. The highest average income from these sources was in J&K (Rs. 5500), followed by Punjab (Rs.4960) and Kerala (Rs.4004). The lowest average income was in Orissa (Rs.1060). The share of different sources of income shows that wages in total income out of four sources was 39 per cent for farmers in rural India and highest being 62 per cent in Rajasthan, 53-54 per cent in Orissa and Tamilnadu, 50 per cent in Kerala and 43 per cent in West Bengal. In all other States, income from cultivation exceeded wage income in farmers house holds.

The size-wise classification of farmer house holds shows that farmers with land size up to 0.01 hectare get their income mainly from wages (Rs.1075) and very little from cultivation (Rs.11). The income from cultivation increases for house holds with a land size of 1 to 2 hectares and above. It is also interesting to note that at the all India level, the income from all the four sources for estimated 78.8 million (88.2 per cent) farmer house holds out of estimated 89.4 million farmers house holds with a farm size up to 2 hectares falls much short of the their total consumption expenditure. Hence most of the marginal and small farmers are indebted and remain in economic misery. This is more or less true for all the States. The income besides from cultivation and wages is very meagre. The size of the land of majority of the farmers (80 per cent) is sub-optimal to derive the income to cover their consumption expenditure. How to increase size of the land to optimal level or to generate other sources of income is the main issue of the income policy for farmers.

Major Challenge

Thus at the close of the 20th century, the biggest problems which are faced by farm sector and the farmers are sub-optimal size of farms, falling or static prices of the agri-produce and dependence of farmers on food grains production besides the problems of scattered small farmers with very small rural population of many villages and lack of organizational capabilities to bring them together or link them with medium and large farmers to expand the size of the farms. Linking of farmers with the agro-processors to transfer the benefits of better marketing and assured demand has emerged off late. Private corporate sector has started experimenting with agreed supplies at remunerative prices with the farmers to be mutually beneficial. However, as the production units of processed agro-products are located in urban areas the benefits of backward and forward linkages are weak to transfer benefits to rural areas. Income transfer mechanism from urban areas to farm sector is still not round the corner.

The major challenge is to transfer income to farmers whose farm size is not adequate to provide them income above poverty line or provide good living standard. The rural sector provides primary commodities for use in the urban sector for processing or direct consumption. But expenditure of urban sector does not reach rural sector as commodities needed are not produced in the rural areas. Rural economy remains as small centres of producing primary agricultural commodities that hardly provides good living standard. The resources flow is largely from the government investment in rural areas. But due to corruption and other leakages not much reaches in rural areas. The gross capital formation in farm sector is merely 1.3 per cent of GDP. There are very meagre alternate employment opportunities in rural areas on which the marginal and small farmers can fall back. In the absence of this, their economic condition hardly improves. If due to economic desperation and financial crisis farmer sells the land, he is reduced to land-less labour or makes exit to urban areas in search of job. This is the scenario of the farm sector and the marginal and small farmers in particular. In spite of spectacular increase in agricultural production and productivity, farmers continue to be in financial crisis.

The important issue to be tackled in the context of marginal and small farmers is to increase the size of their land collectively and develop institutional mechanism that will make them collectively market their produce to get higher incomes. Farmers will have to be convinced and initially may need financial incentives to be partners in production and marketing that will benefit in time to come. This is also essential as the old generation of farmers will be replaced by a new generation of farmers who will see and realize the benefits of higher income and professionally managed voluntary group farming. This aspect is considered in the next Chapter.

Chapter 3

Partnership Farming: Farm Gate Agro-Industry Collaboration

As analysed in the previous Chapter, the main problem in the agriculture sector is assured and sustained increase in farmers' income. The present marketing system under APMA is not farmer friendly, government support and intervention to provide remunerative prices is far from satisfactory. Overall government investment in capital formation in agriculture has not increased adequately to generate economic activities in rural sector compared to infrastructure investment in 1970s and early 1980s. These micro and macro level factors are inherent constraints of the agriculture sector of the economy that will need a new look and policy to introduce changes to correct these constraints. The economic limitation of small size land operation is the main challenge of the 21st Century to get adequate and sustained increase in income. That calls for structural, organizational and institutional changes in managing the farm sector in India.

Charting Farmers' Limitations

As stated earlier the main issue is very low or poverty level income of marginal and small farmers numbering 92.82 million (80 per cent) cultivating 58.8 million hectare (36 per cent) of land. How to raise their income year after year on a sustained basis is the main problem of the Indian economy.

What then can be income raising opportunities for the marginal and small farmers ?

In order to avoid the disadvantages of the small farms, there is need to find out how the production planning can be brought about over a large contiguous area amongst the small farms and medium and large farms on a partnership basis so that economies of scale and efficiency in production can be achieved that will benefit both the groups. Related to this is the marketing of the produce collectively to benefit all the farmers. The only way to increase the size of the farms is to find out the tools to encourage voluntary partnership farming and marketing and generate more on-farm and off-farm employment opportunities.

The partnership needs to be encouraged between the corporate sector and the farmers. Committed partnership between farmers and corporate sector will provide assured demand and price to the farmers and private sector investment in providing the requisite inputs to the farmers will increase the quantity and quality of the produce. This two way mechanism of production has demonstrated the benefits to sugarcane farmers under the cooperative sugar factories where such a partnership benefits the marginal and small farmers as well. Off late private corporate sector has also entered into such partnership with farmers to provide support to farmers through assured purchase of their produce at remunerative prices and providing them with quality inputs. The major initiative commenced from multinational PEPSI in 1980s to the latest one of Reliance.

Private Sector has taken initiatives to develop and tap market of agriculture produce at the door steps of the farmers. The private sector is attempting to establish a two way relation between producers and the consumers through the agro-industrialists of the private sector. This is to provide assured market and prices to all farmers irrespective of the size of the holdings. This farmer friendly approach of the private sector, though in its infancy, is development in the right direction. The private sector initiatives have taken various forms and are at the experimental stage. The major initiatives of the private sector are detailed below.

6.5 lakh Indian villages with vast geographical dispersal have farmers with average size of holding at 1.5 hectare compared to 500 hectares in USA. Small farmers generate small incomes. Size of his produce is small and he has hardly any capacity to hold his produce for better prices. Market is not friendly to him. What market revolution will help him is the real issue ? It is here that some private sector corporate giants came up with novel schemes that were taken to the farmers directly. The profit is the motivating factor for the corporate sector and the farmers. Both are to benefit; farmer getting better price for the produce and assured demand and inputs at less cost and corporate sector to get assured supply of quality agriculture produce.

Corporate Sector Partnership: A Showcase

The first entry in farm sector of corporate sector dates back to late 1980s when the entry of *MNC PEPSI* was made conditional to investment in food processing and farming. PEPSI set up tomato processing plant of 35,000 tonnes importing it from Italy to Punjab in July 1989. The company developed new variety of tomato improving the quality and quantity, processing and reformed the payment system to farmers. Production of tomato in Punjab increased from 16 tonnes to 52 tonnes per hectare by 1994. Though market prices dropped due to increased production, the income of the farmers increased due to substantial increase in productivity. Later PEPSI sold the plant to HLL in 1995 and has moved to citrus plantation. The new venture is PEPSI'S Tropicana Juices. The company is planting one lakh citrus saplings by end 2005 in Punjab. The number is estimated to increase to two lakh saplings by 2007. The company is now entering into sea-weed cultivation in Andhra Pradesh.

This PEPSI Model has set the ball rolling bringing in more initiatives from Indian corporate sector. The Indian companies understood the benefits of linking farmers to processing industries that benefited both. *Indian Tobacco Company (ITC)* developed a more participative model for farmers by linking them to Company through internet. The assembly of elder farmers known as Chaupal (village square) is the hub of rural markets in selling their produce to farmers in an organized manner for mutual benefits. Such **e Chaupals** have started working in 30,000 villages covering about 3 million farmers without government support. This started with Soyabean farmers in Madhya Pradesh. e Chaupals of ITC help farmers in best farming techniques, information about daily weather conditions and prices prevailing in different markets.

The e Chaupal operates a computer with an internet connection with solar operated batteries. Thus information flows to farmers in villages which have no rural roads and electricity. Local farmer trained by ITC works as Sanchalak (Conductor) and operates computer on behalf of ITC and exclusive for farmers. For 50 Chaupals ITC appoints a Sanyojak (Coordinator) who is either a farmer or trader or local dealer of ITC. This institutional arrangement is self financing. For every quintal of produce sold to ITC from e Chaupal, the Sanchalak gets Rs.5. In 2003-04, ITC paid to Sanchalaks about Rs.5 crores as commission. By shifting to Chaupals farmers save about 68 per cent of the costs and processing company about 36 per cent. One e Chaupal covers five to six villages a day and at this rate ITC is covering 30 to 36 villages a day. ITC has so far invested Rs.125 crore and plans to invest Rs.1000 crore.

The e Chaupals are mutually beneficial to farmers and the Company. It is win-win situation thereby eliminating the costs arising out of intermediaries in local markets. In 2000-01 ITC purchased 60,000 tonnes of crop through e Chaupals. By 2003-04 ITC purchased 2.10 lakh tonnes of farm produce and in the next four months lifted 1.80 lakh tonnes. The farmers are drawn to Company due to better prices and also as company weighs on electronic scales which is more reliable, better quality testing and getting spot payment. As ITC puts it "It is transforming the low-knowledge, low-productivity, low-income farming to one of information based, high-productivity and high-income agriculture." It is not just the ITC that gets benefits but how much the farm sector can be transformed.

More and more private sector companies are entering in the rural market sector to connect it to processing industries directly and to consumers indirectly. *Bharati Group,* a Mobile Phone Co., has entered into agreement for a joint sector venture with de Rothchilds of Europe to set up $ 50 million (Rs.225 crore) Field Fresh Foods. The company will export fresh fruits and vegetables to Europe, south-east Asia, middle East and CS countries. It will be getting the produce from farmers of Punjab, J&K, Himachal Pradesh, Haryana, Western Uttar Pradesh and Uttaranchal.

Tata is in farm business for quite sometime. Recently it organized its *Kisan Kendras as Tata Kisan Sansar (TKS)* evolving as one point shops for farmers providing from inputs to loans to marketing. With its 421 centres–all franchisee run–in three States are linked to 20 hubs. Company undertakes contract farming on 15,000 hectares for growing paddy and vegetable seeds in U.P. and Punjab and fruits in

Karnataka and Maharashtra. The produce is sold to retailers and exporters.

Hariyali Kisan Bazaras of DCM Shriram is yet another attempt to reach farmers at their door steps. It caters to farmers' needs by storing 400 types of products from stock feeds, seeds to farm implements. Technical know-how is provided free of cost to farmers and are managed by agronomists. This helps enhancing productivity of the farmers.

Agri-business of Godrej of about Rs.1000 crore under two companies–Agro-Vet and Goldmohar foods deal in animal feed, natural pesticides, and farm inputs. The scheme under the name of *"Adhar" (Support)* is a retail project that provides help to farmers such as soil analysis and veterinary care. Another Scheme *"Manthan" (Churning)* deals in supplying quality animal feed for dairy and poultry which helps farmers in increasing their income.

K K Birla Group under its Chambal Fertilizers and Chemicals (CFCL) has entered in to agri-business through its *Scheme "Uttam Bandhan" (Excellent Contact)* for farmers by training local unemployed youths (Krishi Sevaks). In food processing area it has entered into a unit in Haryana in 2002. The unit processes fresh vegetables and markets under the brand name Ever Fresh.

Another corporate sector company which has entered in agri-business to help the farmers to increase their income is *Mahindra and Mahindra (M&M)* and has network over eight States. Three centres are run by M&MA and rest are franchisees. It has developed oilseeds and cereals and is entering into horticulture. It has entered in contract farming over a lakh hectares. It helps farmers in getting loans through its *Mahindra Krishi Vihars (MKV)* from the banks at lower interest rates. This facilitates banks to increase their business with the farmers through MKVs.

EID Parry's Indiagriline is in agri-business with farmers in 271 villages in Tamilnadu through its Parry Corners (PC) providing advisory services, finance facilities and other support. With the positive support of the farmers the PCs are being transformed into sugar focussed activity.

Reliance's Ralicare set up rural medicinal and herbal plants farming from 2001 with an investment of $5 million. It has developed a 200 hectare herbal farm. Reliance plans to invest another Rs.1000 crore with an eye on supplying herbs to pharma companies.

The number of private corporate sector companies going into agri-business will increase in time to come benefiting the farmers in remote rural areas. This is a new area where modern information technology and the gadgets will help in by-passing the lack of rural roads and electricity and approaching the customers of their produce with the help of corporate sector. What is needed is a Consortium of Corporate Sector with a long term investment plan over a period of 10 years to bring small farmers closer to agro processing industries. This partnership would lead to increase in farmers' income on a sustained basis. Government will have to device incentive package to induce more and more corporate companies to establish network with farmers. Private sector is motivated by profits. If their profits would increase they will increase their participation more aggressively that will benefit the farmers also.

The efforts and the initiatives of the corporate sector are commendable for providing assured demand for agri-produce and thereby increase income of farmers in general and marginal and small farmers in particular. Market information to farmers is crucial to know what their produce can fetch to them in the market and can work as an incentive to increase production and productivity. Farmer gets discouraged when he finds that in spite of increase in production and productivity he does not get the adequate price for his produce. This is especially due to market uncertainties, market imperfection and his weak position as a small producer. The efforts of the corporate sector are drop in the ocean unless government comes out with a package to provide further incentives to increase partnership with the farmers.

In addition to above efforts, much needs to be developed as a coordinated and sustained mechanism to provide assured demand and market support to farmers directly and indirectly. The increased income has to be an outcome of mechanism of production and favourable marketing for farmers. It has to be an inbuilt mechanism and not sporadic. Some of the successful experiments will have to be expanded and new will have to be initiated and operated with the cooperation of the farmers. Farmer centric and farmer supported systems of production and marketing will be durable arrangement.

Partnership Farming in Production and Marketing

The need has arisen to bring the farmers together producing a particular commodity to decide in advance of the season about the item and the volume of production. This is especially important where production is exceeding the demand. Commodity specific Councils or Boards run by the farmers supported by the government in the initial stages with the support of agriculture experts may be the first step. Common Organization of Agriculture Markets (COM) were set up in the European Union (EU) which stabilized markets, secured supplies, protected farmers from fluctuations in the market and encouraged production and productivity. Similar arrangement will be useful to Indian farmers.

India has large number of marginal and small farmers scattered over large areas. In this case, partnership amongst the farmers will have be based on partnership amongst all the farmers of the village or the group of villages and at the all India level amongst the producer of a specific agri-produce such as rice farmers, wheat farmers, cotton farmers and so forth. Thus the Partnership Farming (PF) at the all India level is to be at commodity level and at the local level it will be all farmers (marginal, small, medium and large) producing that commodity. The all India level commodity PF with assessment of demand and supply will send signals to the local level farmers' units as to how much is to be produced and suggest diversification or alternative use of land so that prices received by farmers are remunerative to them. The partnership amongst different size classes of farmers can be either limited to production or marketing or combination of both. Another approach can be purely commercial and managerial where farms can be managed by professional managers and experts and farmers become the share holders.

Production Partnership

Farmers can form a group at the local level for what all is to be produced and in what quantity based on the assessment of over all level of production matching with the demand. The production plan at the local village level is integral part of the macro production plan at the all India level. In this case farmers are free to sell their produce in the market and get the income that should be adequate to repay loans and give them a good reasonable standard of living. In this case role of government will be to intervene through support prices and purchase of produce if the prices in the open market are below the support prices. This will be on the pattern of European Union policy of intervention-storage of such produce at support prices. Production Planning Partnership (PPP) amongst different size class of farmers would help them in protecting their income.

Marketing Partnership

Another partnership amongst the farmers can be limited to marketing of produce. In this arrangement, farmers will decide what and how much to produce independently but will form partnership arrangement in marketing the produce collectively. In the post harvest time, farmers at the local level will be collectively offering their produce in the market that will fetch the best price to them. There can be intra farmers sell of produce *i.e.* small farmer selling his produce to the large farmer at a price which he considers best or at mutually agreed price. Since the holding capacity of the small farmer is meagre or limited, he is exploited in the market. This arrangement can be helpful to sell the produce to large farmer whose holding capacity is better and has access to the market more easily. The best marketing partnership would be to collect all the produce of the farmers and get a good price. In that case good storage, weighing and safety of the produce will have to be ensured by the body of farmers who will run marketing partnership with proper government supervision or by corporate bodies who will have purchase arrangement with the farmers. It is the marketing which is crucial to get proper return to the farmers. Once the marketing partnership starts working satisfactorily, the production partnership can also be brought about to keep a proper balance between demand and supply.

Farmers' Holding Companies: Commercial and Management Approach

The farmers of different size classes can consider setting up a Holding Company or a Partnership Company on the pattern of industrial concerns where the partners bring their share of capital. In case of the farmers' Agriculture Holding Company (AHC), share holders will be the farmers. The access to shares of AHC should be restricted to local farmers/landholders who will be prepared to lease land to the company on long terms basis against issue of shares. AHC should have the arrangement to include all farmers of a village or clusters of villages. The value of the share can be the value of piece of land which the farmer owns or the land taken on lease. The main function of the AHC would be to produce, manufacture and sell agricultural and allied products and is to be managed by the Board of Directors elected by the share holders. The actual production planning and marketing is to be arranged by professional managers amongst the farmers or outsiders chosen by the farmers and experts associated in AHC.

Such an attempt can be made by corporate sector companies who are already in the agro-processing field. Small farm holders will have the advantage of assured income on their share of land as also to work on the farms and get remuneration for their manual or managerial labour. The rules and regulation for operating AHC can be formulated by the government so that arrangement is standardized and to safeguard the interests of small and medium farmers. Such AHC can commercialise farming sector in a big way and help increase private sector investment in capital formation in agriculture. AHC will be collectively managed and self sustaining institutional arrangement that will benefit the farmers. It will have a lot of demonstration effect once the farmers realize the benefit of commercially managed agriculture. This approach to farming will also generate lot of non-farm managerial functions providing employment to rural youths. If this farming is linked to agro-processing, the spin off effect will further increase the non-farm employment. Income flow in rural areas will further improve. The Peoples' Republic of China has experimented with Land Share Company for farmers. It mainly focussed on taking land use rights back from individual households and organizing farmers to form joint stock companies. The land held by the Company could be leased for both agriculture and commercial purposes. The Company system can also help to promote sectoral dèvelopment by moving resources to the efficient producers within each sector and by moving workers from agriculture to other sectors.

AHC will open the area of agro-processing to the benefit of the farmers. AHC can generate high income for farmers, large and stable market for agriculture produce, reduction in wastage and increased employment opportunities. The Food Processing Policy 2005 of the Government of India is highly favourable for such institutional arrangement. Participation and partnership with banks and other financial institutions can help setting up AHC and running it successfully. Lot of incentives given to the agro-processing industry can be integrated with farm gate processing units under the Food Processing Policy and become part of AHC. Enlightened farmers and men with proven track record of organizing farmers can help in setting up model AHCs.

Management of AHC

Some format for setting up AHC can be suggested. It can be set up under the Companies Act as land share company in agriculture based on land stock share system. The share holders should be mostly local land holders who will lease their land to the company on long term basis against the shares. Some cash amount can also be collected from share holders. This can be decided by farmers and the company. The functional area of the company can be either a village or group of villages. The value of the share can be determined on the basis of the market value of land. The company will be run by the elected Board of Directors on a commercial basis. Voting rights of the share holders are to be decided by the Board of Directors. Its function would be to produce, process, manufacture and sell agriculture and other agro-products. Some minimum return on capital can be fixed. Each share holder will receive a share in total profit of the company in proportion to his share holding. The land share is to be transferable to the successor of the share holder. The shares are not to be traded on the market. Otherwise non-farming companies will try to take over AHC.

If the company decides not to undertake farming directly, it can enter into agreement of contractual cultivation with share holder and company will get fixed rent from the farmer and will have first claim on the produce. Company will provide assured market and also provide inputs required by the farmer. In order to encourage the formation of AHC, concessional credit and other investment incentives available to agro-processing companies should be available to AHC also. The company should have the right, in consultation with share holding farmers, to use part of the farm land to develop industrial site and other infrastructure for the purpose of business. This will help in setting up agro-processing units at the farm gate that will generate employment and income in rural areas. The NGOs and Cooperatives which will help in organizing and monitoring AHC can be given development grants. This novel organizational set up will help consolidation of land on a voluntary basis and commercialise the cultivation of agriculture land. The limitation of small size of land can be obviated through the working of AHC.

Contract Farming

Contract farming to share the gains of partnership between the land holder and the industry is not new. It is operating in formal and informal form in sugar and textile manufacturing. The cooperative sugar factories in Maharashtra is a classic example of formal contract farming which benefited the small and other farmers. This is prevalent in some private sugar factories. In textile industry also some private textile mills have contract farming arrangement with farmers for supply of quality cotton.

FAO guide "Contract Farming: Partnership for Growth" states that "the well managed contract farming has proven effective in linking small farmers and profitability for Sponsors". Contract farming reduces the risk and uncertainties of both the parties and provides the opportunities to add value to his production. The main advantage is that the sponsor will undertake the purchase of all produce grown of specified quality and quantity at pre-determined price. The contract also provides improved methods and technologies to farmers because the sponsor has direct interest of improving farmers' production. Sponsors also sometimes indicate in advance the prices to be paid and are specified in the agreement. Government of India is finalizing Model Contract Farming Agreement to give push to Contract Farming for the benefit of the farmers.

The main merit of the Contract Farming is that the sponsoring company undertakes to purchase all the produce of a specified quality and quantity at pre-determined price. This enables the farmers to get technical, managerial and extension services which benefits the small farmers. The sponsoring company invariably offers improved methods of cultivation because it has direct interest in improving the production of the farmers. This enhances the skills of the farmers and they understand the importance of quality production which gives them higher prices for their produce. This system further leads to agro-processing and producers and sponsors achieve economies of scale which brings down the cost of production and making them more competitive.

Of course there are risks in contract farming which may harm interest of the farmers. Sponsors may not adhere to their contact terms. It can result in over production and some sponsors may manipulate the quality standards to reduce purchases. A serious problem arises when farmers break the contract and sell their produce at higher prices in the market. In order to avoid these pitfalls and to develop healthy contractual relationship some arrangement will have to be in position besides the standard guidelines in this connection. The specifications can be laid down for marketing, inputs, credit, production management, delivery and grading system, duration of contract for contract farming agreements. The important factor is the price that is to be calculated which is to be fixed at the start of each season or flexible prices based on open market prices and procedure for payment to farmers. There will have to be legal frame work for Registration of Contract Farming Agreement. The Ministry of Agriculture is in the process of finalizing the Model Contract Farming Agreement and Law to this effect.

It will be clear from the above that various arrangements of Agreement Farming can co-exist depending on the socio-economic development of the areas. What suits Punjab may not suit Bihar or some other State. But basic ingredient of Agreement Farming is to bring the farmers having different sizes of land in a formal arrangement to get the benefit of economies of scale, assured remunerative prices to farmers, improve quality of the produce and make the Indian farmers more competitive in the market. In developing the above institutional arrangements of Partnership Farming what is required is the public information campaigns, farmers' participation and above all consensus building. NGOs can play very effective and vital role in this connection. In fact there are virtually no NGOs in this area. Government can think of giving support and sponsoring and diverting some NGOs in building up different types of Partnership Farming.

Mutual Land Trust for Farmers MLTF)

It may be mentioned that when small investors with their limited knowledge of financial markets could not get adequate return on their savings, government set up Mutual Fund Agency i.e. Unit Trust of India (UTI) which consolidated the savings of very small savers. UTI invested on behalf of the small investors to earn good return to them which they could not have managed to get individually. On similar lines if Mutual Land Trust for Farmers (MLTF) are encouraged in cooperative and private corporate sector who would offer guaranteed income (average of last three years to start with) plus rent of land taken on lease in pre-sowing stage initially for a period of three years. There can also be arrangement to share income when MLTF earns extra profits if market prices are much above the MSP. This can be revised every year mutually on a periodic basis. The post-dated cheques in the name of the farmer can be issued by the cooperatives or private corporate sector for guarantee of agreed income to the farmer. The cheques can be enchased on the due date which should be normally at the start of the harvesting season. That will leave farmer with no botheration of managing the production and marketing it. He can then concentrate earning income from other sources such as live stock, fishing and even wage paid employment on his own farm or other farms.

The MLTF of the cooperative and private corporate sector can arrange the production on commercial lines without any hindrance and at the same time associating the farmers in agriculture production to gear them in production and marketing techniques. In this new strategy the lead will have to be taken by the expert organizers of cooperatives and private corporate sector, marketers and investors so that under MLTF there is increase in the size of land cultivated for assured and sustained increase in farmers' income. Actual nitty- gritty of MLTF can be worked out for implementation.

Farm Gate Agro-Industries

In the absence of employment and income generation opportunities on the farms and in the rural sector in general, the marginal and small farmers on many occasions sell their land and migrate to urban areas where they find opportunities of self-employment in service activities and wage paid employment in industries. The gravitational force in this case is the employment opportunities and not so much the possession of asset. If the commodities produced by the farmer can provide opportunities of income generation at the farm gate farmer can participate in such activities and earn extra income. Instead of farmers and agri-labour moving to urban industries, it will be much more beneficial to bring industries to farm gates. Sugar mills set up near the sugarcane areas is prime example of farm gate agro-industrialization benefiting the farmers in raising their income and employment opportunities. There are other agro-commodities which can pull industries at the farm gate such as food and fruit processing and bulk marketing centres for urban areas. It is the location of industries at farm gate that is important when rural areas can not be depopulated unlike the developed countries.

But the industries do not gravitate to farm gate because of lack of infrastructure facilities. It is the non-commodities part *i.e.* roads, transport, trained labour etc which is very weak in the rural areas. Much of the government resources fail to develop this non-commodity part due to leakages in implementation. On account of this, though the farm sector is the sole provider of agri-commodities at the farm gate, deficiency in non-commodity part fails to utilize the commodities for more income and employment generation. The fiscal system of the government is still not geared to compensate this non-commodity deficiency through fiscal incentives to private sector to set up industries at the farm gate. Initially location of industry at the farm gate may not be financially rewarding. But if sufficient financial incentives and concessions are granted to compensate the private sector to move agro-industries to farm gate, farmers will benefit greatly through accelerating economic activities in rural areas.

The package of incentives to private sector will have to be comprehensive and rural based. Since there are lot of leakages in the implementation of government schemes in rural areas, the package of incentives to private sector will have to be comprehensive. The private sector will have freedom to invest in non-commodities areas that the agro-industries need for setting up such units at the farm gate. This can be worked out and concessional finance to such units and tax holidays of long duration, say ten years, can be thought of.

Circular and Cluster Strategy (CCS): Economic Land-scaping at Farm Gates

The package of concessional finance and tax incentives is be designed in such a way that it works in circular and cluster fashion. Higher the incentive package for farm gate industry if it goes farther into rural area and covers more cluster of villages. This will have economies of scale and larger catchment area to generate more income and employment opportunities to farmers. The entry of private sector in a big way will open the doors of economic landscaping of rural areas that will bring urban facilities and products at the door steps of farmers. Due to very low income and expenditure levels of majority of farmers the market is the limiting factor. Circular and cluster strategy of economic landscaping through private sector entry in a big way can do away leakage of government spending under different programs. The farm sector will diversify from mere manual labour to various steps of agro-processing to marketing. This urban-rural linkage at the farm gate can be a singular most important strategy for location-specific income and employment generation.

This strategy is to supplement the efforts of the current policy of agro-processing of the Government of India. The present concession and promotional measures of the Ministry of Food Processing is encouraging the food processors in the private sector without much emphasis on location of such industries in the rural hinterland. Except the linking of farmers to processing industries through contract farming the rural farm gate linkage is not particularly strong. Unless location-specific linkage of processing industry is established the income transfer mechanism will continue to be very weak. The Circular and Cluster Strategy (CCS) is more oriented to increase income and employment opportunities at the farm gates for the benefit of marginal and small farmers.

The basic principle of CCS is to transfer private sector corporate resources to processing agri-commodities processing as near to farms as possible and simultaneously boost and upgrade the non-commodity part of rural infrastructure *i.e.* roads, transport, communications and improvement in overall landscape of rural areas. The objective is to make clusters of farms as centre of development rather than one way traffic of flow of agri-products to processing in urban areas. Transferring agri-produce for processing in urban areas is only one time backward linkage without much spread effect for income and employment generation on a sustained basis for farmers. When the incentive package can bring the private corporate sector at the farm sites in rural areas for processing then only farmers will be benefited in the short and long run.

India's rural sector is a case of large population with small land holding which is the only resource as means for livelihood at the subsistence level for majority of the population. The sources of return flow of income from urban sector is very meagre and hence perpetual poverty in rural areas that drives hoards of people to urban areas in search of employment and income generation. CCS is to make farm sector as the hub of economic activities through agro-processing located at the clusters of farmers rather than in urban areas. Private sector has shown the resilience to move to farm sector for procurement of agri-produce for processing industries. The need is to take them one step further for processing in clusters of farms.

CCS can change the economic landscape of farm sector in India to benefit the farmers on a sustained basis. It is a matter of changing the direction and gear of government support to private sector to make them rural based for processing activities. Private sector in this case will develop their own marketing and rural knowledge centres on a self financing basis as some of them have already done which has been detailed above.

Radial Farm Gate Industrialization Approach

CCS can be operationalised through radial income generation processes by giving financial incentives and package of tax concessions to corporate private sector for setting up processing units at the clusters of farm gates. Farther such industries go to farm clusters in rural areas, higher should be such a incentive package. This radial location base approach is shown in the following Diagram. Since the farms are of small size the income generated is not enough to provide good living standard on a sustainable basis. Hence there is need to have a sustainable extended means of income from agro-processing in rural areas. The linear growth of agro-based industries in urban areas using agri-produce gives income to urban people. Therefore, the need to have farmer centric rural location based agro-processing for more income to the farmers. Radial approach is geographical spread of argo-based industries from cluster of farms to urban areas so that spin off effects of employment and income generation are internalised. If farm size can not be increased extended agro-processing in the heart of rural areas can achieve the objective of more income to the farmers. This is the ultimate effect of radial farm gate income generation.

Re-Orienting Current Agro-Processing Policy for Farm Gate

The current Food Processing Policy of the government has liberalized the agro-processing. The thrust is to shift to more nutritious diet of fruits and vegetables, milk, meat, fish etc from cereals. The current level of processing of fruits and vegetables is about 2 per cent only and there is vast scope to develop food processing industries. The value of food processing is 14 per cent of manufacturing GDP. It employs 130 lakh persons and has 2.4 times capacity to generate indirect employment. The objectives of government's Draft Food Processing Policy 2005 are to give higher income to the farmers, provide stable markets to them, reduction in wastage and generate direct and indirect employment.

Radial Farm Gate Approach
Agro-Processing for Income Generation

Clusters of Farmers Agro-processing

Structure of Financial Incentives and Tax Concession to Private Sector

Grade I*: Farm Gate (Farther in Rural Areas)

– Highest Financial Incentives

– Highest Tax Concession

Grade II*: Farm Gate (Adjacent to Small Municipality Towns)

– Lower Financial Incentives than Grade I

– Lower Tax Concession than Grade I

Grade III*: Farm Gate (Near Big Sized Corporation Towns)

– Lower Financial Incentives than Grade II

– Lower Tax Concessions than Grade II

– Exact percentage of incentives/tax concession to be decided by respective State/Central Govt.

More concessions to private sector who establish a chain of processing units from Grade I to Grade III.

The initiatives taken by the government are: de-licensing of food and agro processing industries except for some items like beer, potable alcohol and wines, cane sugar, hydrogenated animal fats and oils etc. and items reserved for small scale industries, automatic investment approval upto 51 per cent foreign equity or 100 per cent NRI equity, 24 per cent equity in small scale sector, free use of foreign brand names, relaxation of MRTP FERA regulations, liberalization of import of capital goods and most of the items can be freely imported and exported. Wide ranging fiscal policy changes have been introduced and export-import duty rates have been substantially reduced as also customs duty rates on raw materials. There are tax incentives for new manufacturing units and repatriation of profits are freely permitted. Free Trade Zones (FTZ) and Export Processing Zones (EPZ) have been set up and 100 per cent Export Oriented Units (EPU) in other areas are encouraged. These units can retain 50 per cent of foreign exchange receipts in foreign currency accounts. All profits from export sales are completely exempted from corporate taxes.

It can be seen from the above policy initiatives that there are no specific tax incentives and concessions to set up agro-processing units at the farm gates. The processing policy needs to be rural location based if the benefits of processing are to be derived by the farmers. Lot of direct and indirect employment will be generated if agro-processing policy becomes rural based. This is the major lacuna in the present food processing policy.

Hence, the need to have Radial Farm Gate Agro-Processing so that more and more units are set at the farm gate to benefit the local farmers by generating more employment and income generating opportunities. According to Report of the Research and Consultancy Outsourcing Services (June 2005) on Food Processing Market in India (2005-2010) total food processing goods in India will yield approximately US$ 69.2 billion and value added component will be US$ 22.2 billion. It will attract investment in the form of capital, human, technology and finances to the tune of US$ 32.1 billion by 2010. Considering this phenomenal opportunity, food processing policy will need re-orienting on the basis of Radial Farm Gate Industrialization approach. A package of fiscal and financial incentives will have to be developed by the government.

Unified Farmers' Policy (UFP)

Indian farm sector is beset with marginal and small farmers dispersed over large areas producing small quantities. This denies Indian farmers economies of scale, optimum size of production and ability to withstand the market forces. Besides this, existing agriculture laws have become unhelpful to farmer that affect his costs and income adversely. While the latter are suitably being changed to benefit the farmers, the fundamental structural limitation can be hardly overcome in near future. The farms can not be made big to take advantage of economies of scale and all small farms can not be brought together physically and farm sector can not be depopulated. The income policy is to be evolved under these constraints. In addition, considering the large number of farmers, the direct payment to farmers like that of developed countries can also not be resorted due to tremendous financial burden that will be put on the economy. Subsidies also can not be increased in a WTO environment where the developed countries are under pressure to bring those down.

Given the above limitation the unified policy for farmers can be put into two categories as Pre-harvest and Post harvest instruments supported on four pillars of direct incentives, reducing costs, guaranteed intervention prices much above his cost of production and farm gate agro-processing. Combination of these instruments will help in evolving Unified Farmers' Policy.

Pre-Harvest Instruments of UFP

1. *Financial Incentives for Marginal and Small Farmers for Partnership Farming with Other Farmers*: Financial Incentive can be worked out as certain percentage of farmer's production during the last five years. This production linked incentive can encourage production amalgamated with production by large number of farmers collectively who will be members of such a Consortium. This will protect the farmer from the prospective fluctuations in the current year's production at the pre-harvest stage. This financial addition can be paid to him directly or can be adjusted in reducing the repayment liability of the loan taken by the farmer or in payment of his land revenue. This incentive will directly or indirectly increase farmer' income and also induce him to be voluntary partner in bringing his land under Consortium Farming that will enlarge collective cultivation of land on a partnership basis where each partner can be share holder based on the size of the land that he brings in. He can be further benefited if the inputs such as seeds, fertilizers etc. are purchased in bulk by the Consortium.
2. *Pre-Harvest Sale Price Agreement* can be undertaken by marginal and small farmer for a fixed production quantity with bulk private or public sector agency to ensure income at the pre-harvest stage. Any additional production above the agreed quantity can be sold in the open market. E Chaupal and Village Knowledge Centre can help farmer to quote remunerative price for his produce at pre-harvest stage. This mechanism will provide guaranteed income and also there will be incentive to produce more than the agreed quantity to sell in the open market if the price in the open market is higher than the pre-harvest agreed price. In fixing pre-harvest agreed price, MSP fixed by the government can be taken as the floor price and pre-harvest

price can be quoted 10/20 per cent above this level. Such an arrangement will work as mechanism to get some margin of profit to farmer from the user of farm products in subsequent chain of processing and retailing. Such an arrangement will be beneficial to farmer and agro-processor and add to farmers' income directly.

Post-Harvest Instruments

Post-harvest chain of agri-produce is very vital for enhancing farmer's income on a sustained basis. Large number of marginal and small farmers who add bit of their production in the market are just not aware of supply-demand position of the product in the open market. His self valuation of cost of production and relating it to remunerative price is also rudimentary. He is at the mercy of market forces over which he has no control and his holding capacity is extremely poor. In addition, in the post-Harvest phase due to one time spurt in supply of the agri-produce prices naturally fall which is disadvantageous to him. Under these circumstances farmer needs to be provided explicit support so that increased income becomes available to him and the same is sustained.

1. *Reforming Regulated Markets* for reducing the cost of marketing is the first step in this direction. The present effort of adopting Model APMA by the State governments needs to be urgently implemented so that procedural bottlenecks are eased and costs of marketing are minimized and eliminated finally. But due to well entrenched institutional rigidities and loss of some finances to State governments, it is still difficult to dismantle the existing adverse factors of the regulated markets. The market reforms along with the amendment of Essental Commodities Act (ECA) will free the farmers from the shackles of regulated market regime.
2. *Alternate Farmers' Mobile Markets* can be set up by the private sector. This will save transport and other costs of the farmer. The private corporate sector in the food processing industries can be encouraged to lift agri-produce from the farm gates at the post-harvest stage on a commission basis from local traders who can link farmers and the agro-processing and agro-refining industries such as rice, wheat and Dal mills. This will be beneficial to

farmers and industry to bring about sustained increase in farmers' income and employment generation in rural areas. Initially government can provide financial assistance or tax concessions for a limited period, say three years, to industry to set up such farm gate mobile markets. The local traders and markets in rural areas can be activated by established NGOs.

3. *Supply Management by Procurement Agency* can be useful in guiding the farmers where they should sale their produce to get better prices in the open market and provide them information where they should store their produce to sale it later when the prices will be more remunerative. Procurement Agency can take the produce itself and pay the MSP for some agreed quantity and for the rest of the stock pay higher price realized in the open market later. Procurement Agency working as the trusty of the produce deposited with it can be an instrument for giving more income to the farmers. Rather than making full payment at MSP in one go, it can provide the base payment for sustenance of the farmers initially and later making more payment at high market prices. Stock Receipts from the Procurement Agency can be negotiated to raise loan and financial support from the credit institutions by the farmers for more business.
4. *Para-Agriculture Activities to supplement farmers' income* can be useful instrument to add to farmer's income. This has to be on farm activity in the off season on a continuous basis. In small size of land up to two hectares (about 4 acres), systematic planting of suitable fruits and other trees on the border of the land by the farmer can supplement income. The income generated in this type of para-agriculture activity can work as a fall back income in times of less income from farm.

It is in this context that costing and pricing of agri-produce is important for the farmer which is elucidated in the next Chapter.

Chapter 4

Costing and Pricing in Agriculture: Market and Non-Market Pricing Arrangements

The agricultural economy in India is the biggest private enterprise of small producers. The small and marginal farmers constituting about 80 per cent of the farmers' households bring their small quantities of produce in the market but have very little holding power to get appropriate price for their produce. Not only this group of farmers but the medium and large farmers operating in the open market find that they too do not get proper return to their produce in a situation of surplus production. In such a case, inadequate price intervention by the government results in fall in farmers' income. It is the demand and supply forces that determine the price of the produce. When supply is less than demand farmers get better price for their produce that covers their cost of production generally. But when demand falls much short of production, then the market price falls much below the cost of production and the farmers suffer loss of income.

In order that farmers do not suffer losses and also to provide incentive to farmers to retain land to produce required agri-produce, some arrangement is needed that will cover the cost of production without disturbing the market forces or mechanism. The arrangement has to be such that intervention does not replace the market but should be such that provides cushion to the farmer to protect his income. Before the open market pricing of agri-produce is taken into account it will be useful to understand the non-market pricing arrangement considered to benefit the farmers.

Non-Market Pricing Arrangement

The non-market pricing is the process of fixing prices of agri-produce that will assure the price to the farmer that will cover at least the cost of cultivation. Such pricing is known as Minimum Support Price (MSP) or Guaranteed Price (GP). In India these prices are calculated and recommended to the government by the Commission for Agricultural Costs and Prices (CACP), Ministry of Agriculture. MSP is the floor limit of the price of the produce which covers only the cost of production of the farmer. If the open market price of agri-produce falls below the MSP, it means that farmer is not in a position to recover at least his cost of production. Till the open market price of produce is above the MSP farmer is getting good return on his produce in the market. Higher the open market price than the MSP, higher the gain to the farmer. But if due to fall in demand or due to surplus production vis-à-vis current demand then open market price may fall below the MSP. It is at this stage that the Central Agency intervenes in the market and purchases the produce at MSP to safeguard the income of the farmers. If this intervention is inadequate or falls below the required level, farmers suffer a loss of income.

With the introduction of Green Revolution strategy and more use of fertilizers, high yielding varieties and pesticides and insecticide and increase in irrigation, production of food grains and other commodities increased rapidly. Due to increased supplies the open market prices were threatened to fall. This would have resulted in farmers moving away from the food grains production and also of cash crops such as sugarcane, cotton and jute. Such a situation is not unique to India. In EU countries also surpluses arose for many agri-produce and in order to protect from falling prices a whole mechanism of Support Prices and procurement by government agencies and other subsidies were put in place. When surpluses started arising and open market prices threatened to fall, Government of India under the Ministry of Agriculture set up Agriculture prices Commission (APC) and subsequently renamed now as Commission for Agriculture costs and Prices (CACP).

CACP calculates and recommends to the government Minimum Support Prices on the basis of cost of production for 25 agricultural commodities. Of these 25 commodities MSPs for Sugarcane and Jute are calculated under the Sugarcane and Jute Production Act and hence are known as Statutory Minimum Price. The components/ methodology of calculating MSP adopted by CACP is given below.

Components of MSP/SMP

The components of MSP/SMP are detailed below.

Cost A1= All actual expenses in cash and kind incurred in production by owner

Cost A2= Cost A1 +rent paid for leased-in land.

Cost A2+FL=Cost A2 +imputed value of family labour.

Cost B1= Cost A1+interest on value of owned capital assets (excluding land).

Cost B2= Cost B1 +rental value of land (net of land revenue)

Cost C1= Cost B1+imputed value of family labour

Cost C2= Cost of B2+imputed value of family labour

Cost C2*= Cost C2 estimated by taking into account statutory minimum or actual wage which ever is higher

C3= Cost C2* + 10 per cent of Cost2* on account of managerial functions performed by Farmer

The MSP/SMP is determined by CACP on the basis of C2 cost. To state the components clearly

MSP/SMP= C2

C2=CostB2+imputed value of family labour

MSP/SMP = All actual expenses in cash and kind incurred in production by owner

+ interest on value of owned capital assets (excluding land)

+ rental value of land (net of land revenue)

+ imputed value of family labour

MSP/SMP fixed for 25 agri-commodities covers only the cost of cultivation of the farmer. No margin is provided for farmer's managerial function as is provided in business or commercial activity as profit. The reason for such calculation is stated to be that if higher MSP/SMP is provided inefficient producer will continue to produce that commodity. However, it does not stand to reason why agricultural production should be singled out to treat it as cost based activity and no margin of profit is needed. This is an important issue from the point of view of farmers' income which is being dealt in the Chapter on the subject subsequently.

MSP is an important instrument of Public Food Security System in India. The objectives are to ensure price stability, price support to farmers and provide food grains at affordable price through distribution from surplus to deficit States and to poor. MSP with open ended purchase is within the WTO parameters of liberalization of trade. The MSP/SMP is the floor limit of the return to farmer for his produce and that too it covers only the cost of production as detailed above. In this situation if for any reason the public agency fails to purchase the produce of the farmer and open market price falls below the MSP/SMP, the farmer faces fall in the income. This is what has happened during the last five years for different commodities except oilseeds where production falls short of demand. Farmers, particularly marginal and small, virtually have no margin in returns to his produce which should sustain in times of fall in prices. Even if the productivity has increased for different commodities gains to farmers have not increased commensurately.

The return to farmer per hectare for different commodities with respect to MSP/SMP on the basis of yield per hectare over a period of time is given in Annexure II.

Return to Farmers: Paid out Costs and Imputed Value of Farmers' Land and Labour

The MSP/SMP equals cost of production (C2 Cost) and no profit is provided to farmer. Based on the MSP/SMP and yield of different crops in 2003-04, the highest return per hectare is Rs.48,327 for sugarcane and the lowest for Rs.3878 for Jowar. This is the range of cost-based income of the farmer per hectare at average yield taken for calculations. If the price falls below MSP/SMP and public agency does not intervene or intervenes inadequately and individual farmer's yield per hectare is lower than the average and he has to sell his produce in distress, he will clearly face income loss. MSP/

SMP becomes Support Price only when public procurement agency is operating efficiently to safeguard farmers' income. This is operating successfully for rice and wheat farmers in Punjab, Haryana and UP. Its inadequate support in eastern region has led to sale of rice and wheat below the MSP in open market.

It can also be seen that C2 cost takes into account imputed value of family labour, rent of the owned land and some depreciation. These are not paid out costs but imputed financial value of the items. The later are not incurred or are operational costs. It measures that had he used others' labour and land, that much money cost he would have been required to pay. In fact this margin of not paid out imputed money cost is the cushion of the farmer. So it is his family labour and his ownership of land that keeps his head above the financial crisis when open market price of his produce falls below the MSP/SMP. If this limit stretches year after year he becomes further indebted or accumulates further debt to survive.

Family Labour and Land Owned: Safety Net of Farmers

The money value of family labour, rent of owned land and some depreciation of assets constitutes a significant proportion of total cost of production per hectare for different agri-produce. Since this portion is not the actual out-go of farmers' money it is this portion that sustains him when open market price falls much below the MSP/SMP or his produce is not purchased by public agency at MSP/SMP. In reality, the money value of labour and land component of total cost of calculating MSP/SMP is his own safety net in times of adverse prices in open market or when public agency fails to come to his rescue. The safety margin is shown in the following Table. The commodity-wise details have been calculated on the basis of cost of cultivation data per hectare for the year 2001-02 (latest available) from the Report of CACP 2004-05. The highest and the lowest money value of family labour, rent for owned land and depreciation as percent of total cost are also shown.

The following table reveals the extent of cushion for the farmer in cost calculation on account of family labour and owned land. MSP/SMP does not provide for any additional income for his managerial function. Almost 45 to 50 per cent of the total cost is due to non-paid out money value.

Table 9: Farmers' Own Safety Net

Sl.No.	Commodity	Money Value (per cent) of Family Labour, Rent of Owned Land and Depreciation in Total Cost of Cultivation (2001-02) Lowest	Highest
1.	Rice	27.1 (Kerala)	57 (Orissa)
2.	Wheat	20.5 (Bihar)	51.9 (Haryana)
3.	Cotton	37.0 (Gujarat)	60.7 (M.P.)
4.	Sugarcane	31.6 (Maharshtra)	58.5 (Haryana)
5.	Groundnut	32.2 (Karnatak)	46.6 (Maharastra & Gujarat)
6.	Soyabean	42.8 (M.P.)	47.0 (Rajasthan)
7.	Sunflower	43.0 (A.P.)	64.0 (Maharastra)
8.	Sessmum	39.0 (T.N.)	78.0 (Orissa)
9.	Nigerseed	*	70.7 (Orissa)
10.	Rapeseed & Mustard	31.5 (Gujarat)	75.0 (Assam)
11.	Safflower	*	51.3 (Maharashtra)
12.	Jower	43.5 (Rajasthan)	61.0 (M.P)
13.	Bajra	43.4 (Gujarat)	70.4 (Haryana)
14.	Maize	43.4 (Gujarat)	
15.	Ragi	44.5 (Tamilnadu)	58.0 (Andhra Pradesh)
16.	Tur (Arhar)	45.0 (A.P.)	70.0 (Orissa)
17.	Moong	49.5 (A.P.)	69.3 (Orissa)
18.	Urd	35.3 (T.N.)	70.6 (Orissa)
19.	Jute	57.5 (W.B)	69.3 (Orissa)
20.	Tobacco	*	35.0 (A.P)

* Data for one State only.

Source: Report of the Commission on Agriculture Costs and Prices 2004-05

When does Farmer's Own Safety Net Fail?

If the farmer gets guaranteed MSP he some-how maintains his income to carry on his living out of imputed money value of family labour and rent of his owned land. In fact MSP/SMP does not leave much margin to pay for his past accumulated debts arising out of failure of crops or for some other reasons. The safety net also becomes thin when on his small piece of land (less than a hectare or up to two hectare) his produce falls below the average yield taken for calculating MSP/SMP. His return at MSP/SMP will further go down and safety net becomes thin. It may further become weak when due to surplus production the open market price falls below the MSP/SMP and public agency fails to purchase his produce at MSP/SMP. Since his holding power is very limited he sells in distress his produce at low price in the market leading to fall in income drastically that erodes his own safety net completely. This becomes further critical when he is not paid full sale price of his produce not only by the private trader but even by a government procurement agency. This happened in case of cotton farmers of Maharashtra during the last two years when the government of Maharashtra under its scheme of Monopoly Procurement of Cotton did not make full payment to cotton growers. This led to suicide by the farmers. Thus whole mechanism of non-market prices (MSP/SMP) which is supposed to provide support to farmers in a situation of open market prices falling below the support prices does not rescue the farmers from economic crisis.

Do MSPs/SMPs Cover Minimum Monthly Expenditure of Farmers' Household ?

The Table in Annexure II gives information on return to farmer per hectare at MSP/SMP. When it is converted to monthly income of a farmer's household of 5 members and is compared with the actual expenditure incurred by the farmer HH compiled by the National Sample Survey Organization's (NSSO) 59th Round on situation assessment survey (Jan-Dec 2003) it shows that MSP/SMP falls much short of the income that is required to meet the actual expenditure of the farmers HH.

Based on the CACP data, the average Monthly Per Capita Return (MPCR) for one hectare household farmer for the year 2003-04 from the commodities for which MSP/SMP were fixed works out lowest for Bajra at Rs. 64.6 to Rs. 805.4 for Sugracane. The commodity-wise details of MPCR are given in Annexure II. The average size of the household is taken to be 5 family members based on the NSSO 59th Round. The special survey of situation assessment of farmers conducted by the NSSO 59th Round during Jan.-Dec. 2003 shows that the average Monthly Per Capita Expenditure (MPCE) of farmer's household works out to Rs.502.8. MPCE for 4 per cent of the farmers' households is less than Rs.225.8, for 8 per cent of farmers' HHs it is Rs.300 and for 15 per cent HHs it is less than Rs. 380. At the all India level, Highest MPCE of farmer HH is in Kerala at Rs.900, followed by Punjab Rs.828 and the lowest in Orissa at Rs.341.

The NSSO figures corroborate the fact that MPCR at MSP/SMP of one hectare farmer for some commodities is far below the MPCE reported in different areas. Farmers depending on one crop and depending on rains for cultivation and small marketable surplus survives on his money value of family labour and rent of own land which constitutes a substantial proportion of total cost estimation of MSP/SMP. It is no wonder that marginal and small farmers are almost on the verge of poverty line and face indebtedness. Another Survey of NSSO 59th Round on situation assessment regarding indebtedness of farmers during Jan.-Dec. 2003 reveals that households with one hectare or less land accounted for 66 per cent of all farmers and 45 per cent are indebted. 50 per cent of farmers have taken loan for capital expenditure or current expenditure of Rs.584 out of Rs.1000 of outstanding loan. These findings establish the grim and miserable condition of marginal and small farmers. The farmer is not only caught up in inadequate return from MSP/SMP, he is also confused when he is faced with multiplicity of prices announced by different agencies and open market prices varying at different location.

Multiplicity of Non-Market Prices

Besides the MSP/SMP calculated and recommended for 25 agricultural commodities by the CACP to Central government and later accepted and announced by the government, there are other non-market prices announced by State governments for some commodities. Such prices are not actually calculated by them but are announced on a priori consideration presumably for political patronage and also to give some extra benefit to the farmers. For instance, for sugarcane farmers, State governments of UP, Haryana and some others announce much higher price per quintal than the SMP fixed by the government. There is no scientific basis for this. The sugar factories have then to pay this price to sugarcane farmers. During the last three years the sugar industry has been in the red due to dismantling of controls and reducing levy sugar sell to just 10 per cent as also fall in sugar prices due to bumper production. Due to this the sugar factories could not pay State government announced higher sugarcane prices to farmers. The sugarcane payment arrears touched a record level of Rs. 3500 cro. Such distorting non-market price signals are harmful.

In Maharashtra and other States, sugarcane farmers are paid the price in two stages. First the farmers are paid SMP for a sugar recovery of 8.5 per cent and after the sugar season is over the total revenue of the sugar is arrived at and the profit is shared with farmers on the basis of agreed formula as second instalment of price of sugarcane. In such an arrangement also due to bumper production of sugar and low sales realization the agreed higher price could not be paid. The sugarcane farmers suffered the income loss. In case of cotton, Maharashtra government under its Monopoly Procurement of Cotton Scheme announces very high price for cotton over the MSP which the government sometimes can not afford to pay. Under these conditions no other agency is allowed to purchase cotton and State government due to paucity of funds does not pay the full price to the cotton farmers and arrears accumulate. Recently a number of cotton farmers committed suicide for not getting their dues. The Annexure III illustrates the multiplicity of non-market prices recommended by the State governments. Due to multiplicity of non-market prices the farmers suffer and this affects the production of commodities and income of the farmers. They do not get the proper price signals to decide as to whether they should continue to produce the same item or switch to some other.

The MSPs/SMPs are announced at the time of current harvesting of the produce or when the produce starts flowing to the market. This does not help the farmer to decide whether he should keep producing the same item or move away from it. Once the production comes to the market and due to surplus in production the prices fall in the market. The function of the MSP/SMP as a price or market signal becomes ineffective. CACP has been recommending to the government to announce the MSP/SMP in advance of the season so that farmers can take their decision about cultivating a particular commodity to achieve supply demand balance as also voluntary diversification. Price is a very effective signal for the farmer to get a fore warning for anticipating better return for his produce. There has to be a better coordination between the Central and State governments about the fixing and announcing the non-market prices for different agricultural commodities to avoid wrong signals.

Open Market Price Signal for Production Mix

The supply-demand balance for any commodity is finally reflected in prices that prevail in the open market. Price is a clearing instrument for the producers as to how much the market can take their product. Price changes, therefore, need to be watched carefully to decide about what is to be produced and in what quantity. When the producers are small in size and large in number it is difficult for them to keep track of changing prices reflecting the supply-demand position in the market. This has happened with the marginal and small farmers and farmers in general. Farmers remain so busy with their harvesting activities that they hardly have time to trace the prices beneficial to them and much less in regulated markets.

The movement of prices in the open market for many agriculture produce except oilseeds during the last five years show a depressing trend. The open market price variations are measured by the Whole Price Index (WPI) compiled by the government. The following Table indicates the agri-produce prices in the open market.

Table 10: Open Market Prices: Wholesale Price Index (Base 1993-94)

Item	*1999-2000*	*00-01*	*01-02*	*02-03*	*03-04*	*% Change 03-04/99-00*
Cereals	177.8	**173.0**	**170.1**	173.5	176.3	−0.8
Rice	171.3	**167.5**	**167.0**	**166.0**	169.2	−1.2
Wheat	174.7	176.6	**175.3**	**175.7**	180.7	+3.4
Jowar	240.6	199.7	**182.4**	218.7	**218.5**	−9.2
Bajra	201.2	**184.0**	**151.3**	190.3	**180.1**	−10.5
Maize	193.6	**178.9**	**171.5**	189.5	**181.2**	−6.2
Barley	199.2	**174.3**	**160.2**	193.8	**179.1**	−10.0
Tur	176.3	**150.3**	**142.6**	157.5	172.8	−1.9
Urad	234.0	295.7	**273.9**	**239.8**	**219.9**	−6.0
Moong	180.6	186.9	205.6	208.0	**196.4**	+8.7
Cotton	147.3	157.3	**148.7**	**142.1**	180.0	+22.2
Oilseeds	133.4	**129.3**	137.6	160.2	177.5	+33.0
Ground Nut	139.6	**139.4**	143.4	169.3	180.3	+29.1
Soyabean	107.5	121.2	130.0	153.4	157.5	+46.5
Rapeseed/Mustard	138.7	118.0	126.7	143.4	184.4	+34.9
Sunflower	117.4	118.1	164.0	192.5	193.8	+65.1

Note: Fall in price over the previous year is shown in bold.

Source: Office of the Economic Adviser, Ministry of Industry.

The movement in open market prices of rice and wheat which are major agriculture commodities cultivated by 86.2 million farmers on an area of 70.98 million hectare are facing the problem of falling prices since 1999-2000. The situation is very critical for 35 million farmers cultivating coarse grains where-in the fall in open market price is significant and there is not much support of procurement by public agencies. As the oilseeds are in short supply vis-à-vis domestic demand open market prices show rising trend benefiting the oilseeds farmers.

Open market prices are sending signals to cereals and pulses growing farmers that demand for their produce is falling and surpluses are increasing and it will be beneficial to diversify to some other produce. As these farmers are small and scattered over vast areas and not organized they are not responding to the price signals. Their incomes are declining during last few years. Unlike the developed countries, there is no government agency to guide them in this respect nor Farmer's Commodity Boards to advice them how to respond to the falling prices and get some compensation from the public agencies. Well established Farmers' Commodity Boards are playing very effective role to safeguard farmers' income in developed countries. Commodity Boards managed by farmers and assisted by marketing and other experts guide farmers through production to marketing and fetching higher incomes to them. In open market situation farmers need this kind of assistance in India for sustained increase in income.

Prices and Agriculture Diversification

The above spectrum of open market prices during the last 5 years shows that diversification of commodity production is round the corner. The Budget 2005-06 has come out with the proposal that Ministry of Agriculture is to prepare a road map on diversification of agriculture. Based on the present demand-supply condition with pent up demand for food grains due to lack of purchasing power of large number of poor people, the falling prices of agricultural commodities *i.e.* cereals, coarse grains and pulses need not suggest that the increased production of these commodities is not required and that the land should be diverted to some other produce. What is needed is the slow pace of diversification to other crops, increased procurement by central agency to ensure proper return to farmers and to increase national and international demand for these commodities. Since the oilseeds are in short supply and there is great scope to increase production, land can be diverted to produce more oilseeds to reduce dependence on import of oilseeds. This diversification will increase employment and income of the farmers. Tapping overseas markets for oilseeds and edible oils can make this commodity sector a booming sector in the next decade.

To achieve this, oilseeds farmers will have to organize Farmers' Oilseeds Board or even specific Oilseed Board like that of Soyabean farmers of USA. Such a model is already working in USA and India can draw on their experience suiting Indian conditions. A brief profile of American Soyabean Association (ASA) is given below. Soyabean farmers now have entered in Soya-Diesel production and have been able to increase demand for Soyabean on a sustained basis and commensurately adding to their income. This is a unique model of self help for the farmers to improve their economic well being. Indian farmers can draw on ASA Model.

American Soyabean Association (ASA)

1. Founded 1920. Registered 1925. Incorporated 26th Feb 1946.
2. Soyabean farmers and extension workers founded the Soyabean Association to promote the crop and increase profit appropriation. Early Soyabean farmers agreed that processors would undertake production of 50,000 acres at guaranteed minimum prices. Due to surpluses of wheat and cotton in 1930s Soyabean became an attractive crop that led to increase in production and more profit to farmers.
3. World War II: production doubled. Producers built plants to produce oil. After the war surplus arose. Soyabean was not part of govt. food aid plans.
4. ASA leaders travelled at their own cost to survey potential markets. ASA and Foreign Agriculture Service (FSA) signed joint market development contracts for work in Europe and Japan. Tokyo office was opened in 1956.
5. Farmer funded Check-off Program through sale deduction of 1 to ½ cent per bushel helped farmers. Elected Boards were set up to control funds for market development and research in 1964.
6. During 1980s AS Development Foundation was set up. South American markets were located. ASA set up international offices in 11 countries.
7. In 1990s Market Promotion for Eastern European consumer was started. Soya Diesel and vegetable based printing ink encouraged. Bio diesel B20 as alternate fuel developed. Crop insurance coverage was enlarged.
8. ASA and National Bio Diesel Board (NBDB) obtained Deptt. of Energy agreement to consider B-20 (a blend of 20 per cent bio-diesel made from vegetable oil and 80 per cent petroleum Diesel)) as an approved alternate fuel.

Contd...

Contd...

9. Soyabean Check-off Program: Framers invest their own money in strengthening market demand, improving productivity and increasing profitability. One-half of 1 per cent of the delivered price is deducted for Check-off Program when farmers' sell their Soyabean.
10. Oct. 2004: ASA's major achievement came up when *President George W. Bush signed into law a bill containing the first ever bio-diesel tax incentive.* Passage of bio-diesel tax incentive and extension of ethanol tax incentive was realized as part of H.R. 4520 known as Jobs Creation Act 2004. Tax incentive took effect from 1st Jan. 2005 and lasts for two years. For every 100 million gallons of Soyabased bio-diesel demand, the price of Bushel of Soyabean is expected to increase by 10 cents. That could add an average of another $2000 to the bottom line of farmers growing 500 acres of Soyabeans.
11. Production achieved record level of 3.14 billion Bushels, yield 42.5 Bushel per acre, exports of 1.1 billion Bushel.
12. 2004: ASA had 25,800 members. There are 23 State level Soyabean Associations.

Source: American Soyabean Association Website.

The open market prices for cereals and pulses as also for grains are showing a declining trend due to surplus production and lack of current demand. No public or private agency has come up with any significant model to assist these farmers. There are 86.2 million rice and wheat growing farmers cultivating an area of 70.98 million hectares and 35 million coarse grains farmers cultivating an area of 31 million hectare. If these farmers from their own Commodity Associations or Boards and help each other with the assistance of experts and others on the pattern of American Soyabean Association they can improve their economic condition and increase income on a sustained basis. In India, area under Soyabean cultivation is 5.87 million hectares with the production of 4.56 million tonnes in 2003-04. Large number of farmers are cultivating Soyabean. But enough attention is not received by this crop as can be seen from the fall of yield from 1086 kg per hectare in 1993-94 to 777 in 2002-03. The price scenario for Soyabean is very favourable to farmers as revealed from the open market prices (WPI) increasing by 46 per cent in 2003-04 over 1999-2000. A well organized Soyabean Farmers' Commodity Board or Association can add to farmers' income and improve their economic condition as has been done by the ASA of U.S. Even an assistance can be sought by Indian farmers from ASA to set up Indian Soyabean Farmers' Board (ISFB). Government agency and private initiatives are not adequate to improve economic conditions of farmers but the time has come for farmers to organize themselves to deal with problems of supply demand management on a sustained basis to increase income.

It would be clear from the above that farmers are subjected to multiplicity of prices for reasons of price stability and food security. Price mechanism of food grains is combination of taking step towards more commercialisation of agriculture but at the same time protecting the farmer with the help of MSP and procurement arrangements. A Committee headed by Dr Abhijit Sen, Professor, Jawaharlal Nehru University and now Member Planning Commission studied the existing pricing and procurements in 2002. The Committee has endorsed that the MSP should be continued but should be announced before the sowing so that farmers can take decision about production of agriculture produce. Central government should underwrite open ended purchase of food grains by FCI and involve State governments, private sector and cooperatives. The FCI should shift its focus of procurement of rice and wheat from Punjab and Haryana to Central and Eastern States so that the farmers in those States do not face a situation of open market prices falling below MSP. In order to reduce the cost of holding of food grains, the Committee suggested that early commercial disposal of old stocks may be undertaken and demand for food grains may be expanded through larger public works.

The Committee has mainly provided framework for cost effective management of food stocks and expanding the coverage of FCI and expanded role for private agencies. Given the present arrangement it is farmers of Punjab and Haryana producing rice and wheat in surplus quantity who are the main beneficiaries. Farmers in other States and producing other items are still out side the safety net of MSP and procurement. It is evident from this that the income effect of green revolution in other parts of the country has been weak though their contribution to production is no less important. It is in this context that a comprehensive income policy needs to be devised so that production and productivity of farmer is translated in to increase in income on sustained basis. This is the main theme that has been deliberated in the subsequent Chapters.

Chapter 5

Agriculture Marketing: Institutional and Commodity Reforms

Indian agriculture has now crossed the Rubicon of scarcity of agriculture produce and especially of food grains except for the oilseeds production falling short of demand. With this self sufficiency on the agriculture front it was expected that farmers' income will grow rapidly and the upward direction will be sustained. But at the turn of the century, farmers find themselves in a situation of plenty in agriculture produce vis-à-vis current demand where in prices for their produce are sluggish or falling and markets which were friendly in a situation of scarcity have now put them in difficulty. The macro economic factor also worked against the farmers as the rate of growth of agriculture sector in the recent past has come down to 1.5 per cent resulting in fall in share of agriculture sector in GDP but carrying the same proportion (72 per cent) of population on its shoulders.

Is it that the commercialisation of agriculture sector did not take place adequately or that the supply chain from farm gate to users of agri-produce worked to the disadvantage of the farmers ? Or alternatively open market prices were far from adequate and government announced prices were not remunerative enough to provide sustained increase in his income ? The main issue in the farm sector now is not so much the lack of production and productivity alone but the cost effective and farmer friendly marketing set up and remunerative prices. There is strong network of government institutions such as ICAR, IARI and host of Agriculture Universities and research institutions which help farmers to increase productivity. Hence production and productivity aspects are well taken care of and government keeps updating programs in this area. With little more reorganization, their performance can be improved which the government does periodically. What is important to farmer is post harvest marketing and pricing reform strategies and policies that will benefit him immensely.

There is no denying the fact that increased productivity is key to increased income for the farmers but at the same time prices received for the produce is the vehicle that will fetch increased income to the farmers. The agriculture productivity (yield per hectare) has gone up one and half times to two times during the period 1970-71 to 2003-04. However wholesale prices of agriculture produce such as food grains, sugarcane, cotton and others show a fall in 2003 over 2000. Thus it is not so much the lack in productivity alone but marketing and prices which are responsible for low income of the farmers. The existing marketing arrangements of the agri-produce and pricing mechanism (open market and government announced) seem to be inadequate and need reforms urgently.

Marketing and Price Scenario

The agriculture produce markets are regulated under the Agriculture Produce Marketing Acts of the State Governments. The main objective of market regulation is to ensure that farmers get fair prices and transactions are transparent. APMA empowers the State governments to notify the commodities, markets and market areas that are regulated. APMA also provides for setting up of Agriculture Produce Marketing Committees (APMC) which are responsible for the operation of the markets. They have the authority to levy and collect market fees on all transactions taking place in the regulated markets. There are 7310 regulated markets of which 7161 are covered under Regulation. Of the 27,294 rural markets, about 1 per cent are Regulated markets.

Initially the Regulated Markets (RM) helped the farmers in mitigating hardships at the wholesale stage. However, over a period of time and when production started exceeding the demand, the RMs did not provide requisite assistance in direct and free marketing, organized retailing, assured supply to agro-processing units and innovative marketing systems and technologies. The services such as grading, standardization, storage and financing facilities required for competitive marketing did not develop under the RMs. The overall effect has been increased cost of marketing to farmers and low prices for their produce affecting their income adversely.

The loss to the farmer under the existing APMA due to mark-up at different stages of marketing is illustrated in Table 2 in Chapter I. The table clearly shows that with reform of APMA farmers' losses can be reduced in transportation and wastage by 25-30 per cent. Alternative measure of increase in income is the difference in the farm-gate price to the produce of the farmer and subsequent stages of marketing which is shown in the Table 3 in Chapter I.

The Table shows the price jack up of farm produce from "Farm Gate" to the "Retailer" and finally much more to the "Lunch Table" (consumer). If the farmer is linked, with reform in APMA, to wholesaler directly, he is likely to get increase in income by about 25-30 per cent. But that needs change in APMA of the State governments, which is not forthcoming.

Major Reforms Initiatives

The self sufficiency in food grains and surpluses in other agriculture produce such as cotton and sugarcane showed the limitations of the working of regulated markets under APMA. The Ministry of Agriculture and Cooperation was seized of the inadequate and outdated marketing system of agriculture produce, increased costs to farmers in the supply chain from farm gate to whole sale markets, restrictions imposed on farmers not to sell to user his produce directly, lack of grading and storage facilities to get better prices and other institutional hurdles. The Ministry carried out major reviews of the existing marketing inadequacies of the APMA and appointed the Expert Committee on Strengthening and Developing of Agricultural Marketing (2001) and the Inter Ministerial Task Force on Agriculture Marketing Reforms (2002). The Expert Committee after studying the monopoly of licensed traders in the regulated markets recommended that registration, rather than licensing, with the APMA be sufficient for private traders to do marketing in regulated markets. The Task force recommended that APMA need to be amended to permit direct marketing and establishment of agricultural markets in the private cooperative sector.

Based on the recommendations of Expert Committee and the Task Force, Ministry prepared a Model APMA for agricultural produce marketing to be adopted by the State Governments with requisite modifications. Under the Model Act, private traders can be licensed to set up a market or buy produce directly from farmers. Ministry initiated implementation of Model Agriculture Produce Marketing Act (APMA) by the State Governments and is providing financial incentives to State Governments under Ministry's new Scheme called Development/Strengthening of Agricultural Marketing/Infrastructure, Grading and Standardization. Rs.72 Cro. have been provided in Budget 2005-06.

In addition to this, Amendment to Essential Commodities Act (1935) has been initiated and approval of the Parliament is being sought. ECA dates back to the period when essential agriculture and other commodities were in short supply. It was operated through control on storage, movement and trading in large number of agricultural commodities such as food grains, pulses, sugar and edible oils. Now that agriculture commodities supply has increased, these restrictions are affecting the farmers adversely. The Central government issued an Order in 2001 removing the licensing requirement and all restrictions on purchase, stocking, transporting of specific agri-produce including wheat, rice, oilseeds and sugar. But State governments have also to take necessary steps. Central government is introducing the Bill in the Parliament in this respect. As per amendment of the Act, there will be no permanent list of essential commodities and there will be no restriction on the production, supply and distribution of commodities. This is considered to benefit the farmers to get better prices for their produce. All that the government will do under the ECA is to retain the power to declare an item as essential in times of crisis.

The government has initiated steps for trading in Godown Receipts as a measure to enhance the capacity of the farmer to get better prices for his produce by storage of produce and take it to the market when prices are rising. Negotiable receipts would help farmers to get loans for marketing purpose and farmers can get better prices for their produce. Government is bringing a Draft Warehousing Development and Regulation Bill to make warehouse receipts legally acceptable in the banking system and commodities market. This aims to reduce transaction cost and increase credit flow to the farmers. This will bring gradation, standardization and other services to commodity market benefiting the farmers. This will encourage private sector investment in warehousing and end the monopoly of Central Warehousing Corporation and State Warehousing Corporations. Central Sector Scheme has been launched for construction of Rural Godowns and Cold Storage in rural areas that will facilitate pledge loan to prevent distress sale. This will also promote grading/standardization of farm produce to improve marketability.

Government is also making suitable amendments to Food Processing Laws and initiating legislation for contract farming for friendly marketing arrangements with private sector investment and assured demand for farmers' produce.

Task Ahead: Farmer Centric Reforms

Market reforms detailed above are in the right direction and would pave the way for better return to farmer for his produce. However, these measures are passing through a transition phase from regulated markets to open market situation. This will require lot of adjustment on the part of agri-product users and price paid to the farmers for their produce.

Since large number of farmers are marginal and small farmers their stake in the marketing in changing market environment will need special attention.

As per Agricultural Census 1995-96, out of total 115.5 million operational holdings, 71.18 million (61.6 per cent) are marginal holdings cultivating an area of 28.12 million hectare (17.2 per cent). Such small holdings have hardly any marketed surplus, as it is mostly subsistence level except selling some small quantities in local rural markets. Same is the situation of small farmers. Thus marginal and small holdings numbering 93.8 million (80.3 per cent) cultivating an area of 58.84 million hectares (36 per cent) may not be generating much of marketable surplus except those who have irrigation facilities. In case of marginal and small holdings, it is essential to raise them above subsistence level and bring them in the fold of generating marketed surplus.

Thus from the point of view of agri-produce market, the marketed surplus should be coming from 22.75 million semi-medium, medium and large holdings (29.6 per cent) cultivating an area of 104.5 million hectare (64 per cent). In fact, semi-medium and medium farmers numbering 21.4 million cultivate an area of 80.3 million hectare (59 per cent) who are the back bone of generating marketed surplus besides 1.4 million large farmers (1.2 per cent) cultivating an area of 24.2 million (14.4 per cent). Therefore, changes introduced in the regulated markets and opening of commodity markets and resultant pricing will have greater income impact on semi-medium, medium and large farmers. This should be target group for market reforms for increasing their incomes and bringing 93.8 million marginal and small holdings above subsistence level cultivation.

Commodity-wise Marketed Surplus

The size of the agri-produce market depends upon the marketed surplus that becomes available in the market for sale. Marketed surplus ratio (MSR) of important agriculture commodities is given in Annexure IV. The marketed surplus depends upon the production over and above the subsistence level, availability of transport and connectivity by road to markets. The Annexure shows that for wheat and paddy and pulses MSR ranges between 50 to 80 per cent and similarly for maize. For oilseeds, MSR is over 80 per cent. For sugarcane, cotton and jute 100 per cent. For vegetables (Onions and Potatoes) MSR ranges from 50 per cent to 95 per cent.

Based on above MSR, agr-markets can be broadly classified in three categories (a) Food grains and oilseeds, (b) Horticulture (fruits and vegetables), (c) single end user market *i.e.*, sugarcane, fibres: cotton and Jute and Mesta. The type of market through which the above commodities pass for sale and end user to whom it is connected will determine the price that the farmer will get for his produce which will determine his income.

Therefore, it is important to know the number of farmers producing such of the above categories of agri-products. This will enable us to see the target group of farmers and market in which they operate and reforms needed so that it has positive and sustained impact on the farmers' income. Number of farmers by crops is given in the Table 7 of Chapter II. The Table shows that large number of marginal and small farmers are dependent on food grains and their income levels will depend on the markets where it is sold and the prices that they receive.

Agri-Crop Markets and Price Reforms

Based on the above identification of crop-wise and size-wise target group of farmers, the market reforms and pricing mechanism can not be omnibus. The market reforms and pricing will have to be crop specific or broad group of agri-produce such as food grains and non-food or commercial crops. Too much generalization of market reforms may lose the focus of target group of farmers for whose benefit the reforms are to be introduced. Farmer has to be on vanguard of all reforms along with the increase in production and productivity in farm sector. Farmer and crop centric reforms need to be evolved if the farmer's income is to be protected and increased in a sustained manner in future.

Foodgrains and Oilseeds

Food grains production is the main stay of the farm economy in India. As given in the above Table 7 in Chapter II 137.2 million farmers produce food grains. And over 70 per cent are marginal and small farmers. These farmers produced record level of food grains at 212 million tonnes in 2001-02. Food grains sold in the regulated markets under the APMA of the State governments are subjected to the transaction losses in the range of 35 to 40 per cent. Though food grains marketing is liberalized off late, not many changes have taken on the ground to get adequate returns to farmers. With food grains production exceeding the demand, the open market prices would have crashed drastically but for government purchases at Minimum Support Price. In 2002-03 about one third (27.8 per cent) of wheat production of 69.32 million tonnes and one fourth (20.8 per cent) of rice production of 75.7 million tonnes was procured by Food Corporation of India (FCI). In fact, in rice and wheat marketing at MSP FCI as major player provides stability of income to farmers. This is more in case of farmers of Punjab, Haryana, UP, AP and Chhatisgarh. In the absence of procurement or meager procurement of rice and wheat in Assam, Bihar, Orissa and West Bengal, the prices fell below MSP and farmers in these States were adversely affected.

Now that the rice and wheat will be out from the list of ESA with the proposed amendment, the farmers will be exposed to open market and prices may further fall. Once the food grains market is decontrolled and if the FCI will not be a major player in the market, the farmers will have lot of hardship to protect their income initially. But market surveys and analysis show that MSP is working to the disadvantage of the farmers. Once the markets are decontrolled more purchasers will demand wheat and it is reported that they are ready to offer higher price but in the present situation they pay only the MSP. Farmers are expected to gain in the open marketing of food grains. The position of pulses and coarse grains market will also be in same situation. In case of coarse grains, to increase production MSP were jacked up to grow Maize as a substitute of Paddy where feasible. There are 35 million coarse grains farmers whose future will depend upon the remunerative prices in the open market. The market for coarse grains is highly localized to the States growing these cereals–Jower in Maharashtra and Bajara in Rajasthan.

In regard to oilseeds, more than 12 million farmers are engaged in three major oilseeds namely groundnut, rape seed and sunflower. There is shortfall in the production of oilseeds vis-à-vis demand and the prices in the market continue to be buoyant. In addition, the MSP of oilseeds and pulses were given reasonable hike to increase the production. The MSP and open market price regime has positive impact on oilseed farmers' income. The expected record oilseeds production of 25 million tonnes would provide self sufficiency and reduce dependence on imports. However, there should be no complacency considering the growing demand of edible oils in future. In open market regime, marketing arrangements should be in position so that problems of glut are taken care of well in time.

The market reforms for food grains alone will not be enough. The problem is related to production also. While maintaining and increasing the level of food grains production, number of farmers depending on food grains production will have be diverted to other crops. Number of steps and programs have been taken up by the Ministry of Food and Consumer Affairs for streamlining the working of FCI and for market reforms legislation by the Ministry of Agriculture and Cooperation.

For further benefit of the farmers, Program of Diversification from food grains production to non-food grains needs to be put in position urgently. The Budget 2005-06 has already set the tone by asking the Ministry of Agriculture to prepare Road Map for Agricultural Diversification. Requisite technological and infrastructure and policy support will be required for the State governments. This can be first taken up in Punjab, Haryana and UP so that more farmers move out from rice and wheat to other crops consuming less water. Encouragement for production of wheat and rice can be given to Assam, Bihar, Orissa and West Bengal and increase of procurement by FCI in these States to protect the farmers from falling prices.

Special Market Expansion Package (SMEP) for Coarse Grains produced by 35 million farmers can be thought of. The production and market for coarse grains is highly localized and there is not much support of procurement for these farmers. Coarse grains have good fiber content and are picking up as healthy food in urban areas. Some small home made processing units are making good sale of processed coarse grains in urban markets in Maharashtra. But there is not much of commercialization. The sustainability of coarse grains and livelihood of 35 million farmers can be raised through market expansion by encouraging established food processing companies for advertisement campaign and for finding more domestic and overseas markets.

Horticulture Products: Fruits and Vegetables

India's production of fruits and vegetables shows a phenomenal growth. In a period of ten years (1990-91 to 2000-01) area under cultivation increased from 10.53 lakh hectare to 14.97 lakh hectare (+ 42 per cent) and production increased from 11.46 million tonnes to 20.94 million tonnes (+82.4 per cent). This spurt in horticulture sector has implication for direct and indirect growth in income generation and employment. Though figures of number of farmers in horticulture sector are not available, the growth in production and area under cultivation is indicative of its potential and opportunities to farmers to diversify in this sector.

However marketing has been a weak link in this sector due to inadequate grading and standardization and packaging facilities besides the storage facilities and losses arising out of lack of connectivity to urban markets and costs of post harvesting supply chain. According to the Expert Committee of the Ministry of Agriculture, 30 per cent of horticulture products are wasted every year due to inadequate storage and transport infrastructure. Wastage occurs due to rough handling, inadequate packaging and lack of temperature control.

In order to take care of the marketing problems of fruits and vegetables, government has already moved ahead with suitable amendments to APMA. In order to increase production of fruits and vegetables, government has set up a Horticulture Mission recently and provision has been made of Rs. 630 Crores in Budget 2005-06.

The horticulture production raises two priority issues, one related to income generation and the other being introduction of new vegetables and fruits which have great demand in higher income groups in the domestic markets and as exports. This is a new area to which not much attention has been paid. Much relief to the horticulture farmers will come when the APMA removes costs of marketing in regulated markets.

In addition to the reforms and support measures already in operation, *Fruits and Vegetables Collection Consortiums (FVCC)* of leading food processing companies and also AMUL, SAFAL, NAFED and State level Public and Private Agencies to collect fruits and vegetables at the farm gate will be of great help to farmers. The aggregation of small production will have to be supported by giving tax and other concessions to such players so that costs of the small farmers are reduced and giving an assured income to them. The marketing will have to be initiated outside the regulated market areas and near the farm gates.

Setting up of *Domestic Processing Zones in Rural Areas (DPZRA) for Fruits and Vegetables on the pattern of export processing zones* by the corporate sector will link farmers to urban consumers. This backward and forward production-processing linkage mechanism in rural areas will benefit farmers, urban consumers and corporate sector. Such processors can be deemed exporters and should get all tax concessions and facilities. This will be the first step to process and export from rural to urban markets. The fruits and vegetable farmers may be made shareholders in such enterprises.

Cash Crops Marketing

(*i*) Sugarcane

There are 5.2 million sugarcane farmers cultivating an area of 4.29 million hectare and produced 300 million tonnes of sugarcane. The average productivity is around 680 quintals per hectare. Sugarcane marketing formally and informally is on contract farming basis and sugar mills in the area are captive buyers of sugarcane. Cane farmers sell cane directly to sugar mills. Since the sugar content of the sugarcane is to be extracted as early as possible, it can not be stocked unlike other commodities. The sugarcane farmers are paid on delivery of sugarcane at the Statutory Minimum Price at 8.5 per cent recovery fixed by the government and some additional income to farmers based on the recovery by the sugar mills at the end of the season. Farmers did not face any difficulty in this marketing and pricing arrangement till production of sugar was short of demand and sugar industry was under control.

It is important to note that three types of prices are prevailing for sugarcane. The first one is Statutory Minimum Price (SMP) of CACP approved by the government which is a weighted average price of all the State SMPs. The second set of price is the SMPs calculated for the States but not announced. The third set of price is State Announced Prices (SAPs) of different State governments. The prices paid by the sugar factories published by CACP indicate that these prices are more or less close to the SAPs except in case of Maharashtra. In Maharashtra, SMP is paid to sugarcane farmer in the first place and the additional payment to farmer is done at the end of season on the basis of sharing formula. This arrangement worked more or less satisfactorily till 2000-01.

With the increase in production and productivity of sugarcane and production of sugar exceeding demand from 2000-01, stocks of sugar accumulated to around 10 million tonnes. In addition to this, sale of sugar was decontrolled raising open market sugar to 90 per cent and only 10 per cent under levy. The average price realization from sale of sugar decreased from Rs1335 per quintal in 1997-98 to Rs.1296 in 2001-02. As per the recent market analysis, the sugar prices will range between Rs. 15 to Rs. 17/kg and a combination of politics and good sowing next year will keep them there. This whole process of falling prices led to less sales realization by sugar factories that resulted in delayed payment to sugarcane farmers adversely impacting on their income. The sugarcane arrears are now about Rs.3500 crores.

The Central government is now amending the Essential Commodities Act (ECA) that will fully decontrol the sugar also. This will have impact on the sugarcane farmers further. In that case the SMP for sugarcane may be a reference price. The price paid to sugarcane growers will depend upon the prices which the sugar factories will offer in different States. Since the sugarcane farmers are mostly small farmers they may be adversely affected. Sugarcane farmers do not have their organization to collectively deal with sugar factories. In the light of these developments, Formalizing Contract Farming Agreements can be the first step in this direction.

Price Guiding Forum (PGF) of the sugarcane growers and the sugar mill owners will give a collective forum to take decisions about the supply-demand management and better and assured returns to farmers. This Forum can settle the price of cane before the start of the season in mutual consultation and at the end of the season make additional payment to cane farmers based on agreed sharing formula. This Forum can also work as Sugarcane Arrears Surveillance agency and make the sugar industries pay to cane growers in time. Sugar price movement and its monitoring in the market should be such as to pay the farmers in time to avoid cane arrears. It has been observed that from 1997-98 with accumulation of stock with bumper sugar production and decontrol of sugar, sugar prices remained depressed and even decreased compared to 1997-98 till 2003-04.

While the sugar consumers might have been benefited, realization for sugar factories declined resulting in increased cane arrears. In order to avoid such an eventuality due to production exceeding the sugar demand adversely affecting the cane farmers, a mechanism needs to be developed to work out the price of sugar in the current season to be higher than the previous season by disposing of sugar stock in domestic and international market. Sugar price movement is to be such that there is adequate realization by sugar factories for paying cane farmers their dues in time.

Annual Plan for Export of sugar is required. In order to avoid sugar glut in the market resulting in depressed sugar prices, sustained sugar exports should be planned. This will help sugar industry to plan extra capacity and build markets of sugar overseas. Recently, Commerce Ministry has drawn a plan for export of jute from Rs.1000 cro to Rs. 5000 cro. in the next five years. Requisite incentives will be needed for sugar factories also to produce for exports.

Total proceeds of sugar factories from sale of sugar, molasses (liquor) and bagasse need be taken into account in paying the price of sugarcane. This will give proper share of increased productivity to the farmers that will increase their income. This will work as incentive to increase yield by the farmers.

(ii) Cotton

Income of over 5 million cotton farmers cultivating an area of 7.48 million hectare depends on proper marketing arrangements, pricing and timely payments to them. Maharashtra with 1.92 million cotton farmers leads, followed by Andhra (0.71 million), Gujarat (0.54 million) and Karnataka (0.49 million). These four States account for 3.67 million (73.4 per cent) farmers.

The year 2004-05 has been the worst for cotton farmers due to glut in market that led to fall in prices below MSP and inadequate purchase by government agencies and late announcement of cotton exports. The farmers went bankrupt and many committed suicide. The worst scenario of cotton farmers was in Maharashtra where Monopoly Procurement of Cotton (MPC) resulted in distressed sale. While the cotton was delivered, due to paucity of financial resources and offering much higher price above the MSP, the cotton payment arrears of farmers touched a record level of Rs.6500 cro. in Maharashtra. The arrears have not been paid as late as May 2005. Maharashtra government announced on 10th May 2005 that for the coming season, cotton will be purchased at MSP only. The position of farmers who are in contract with the textile mills is relatively better off but that number is very small. Given this scenario, market reforms and prices need to be in position for the coming cotton season and also for future.

It may be pointed out that the fall in prices has been taking place in the cotton market due to high production in the world market. The stocks fluctuated between 20 to 50 per cent of global output and have affected cotton market considerably. At that stage USA shifted from stock holding to price support from 1985 onwards. According to recent World Bank Study (WB Policy Research Working Paper 3218, Feb. 2004) "prices declined considerably during last fifty years; one-fifth of their 1950 levels." High cost cotton producing country like USA with its policy of subsidizing the cotton production has introduced distortion in the market which affects India along with other countries. Mexico complained to WTO against USA on distortions in the cotton market and has won the case. According to the World Bank Study which focussed on Benic, Minot and Daniels (2002) 40 per cent reduction in farm gate cotton prices, equivalent to the price decline from December 2000 to May 2002, implies a 7 per cent reduction in rural per capita income in the short run and 50-65 per cent reduction in the long run. The average incidence of rural poverty including cotton growers and other farmers rose from 40 per cent to 48 per cent. The suicides of cotton farmers in India is stark evidence of their poverty due to falling prices and inordinately delayed payments.

The cotton market is affected by rapid expansion of chemical fibres, mainly polyester. Polyester prices were four times higher than cotton prices in early 1960s. Following technological improvements they declined to the level of cotton prices in early 1970s and since then polyester and cotton products have been trading at similar price levels. The long term decline in cotton prices has been the result of technological improvements such as application of improved varieties, fertilizers, chemicals and irrigation. Between 1960 to 2000 world cotton production doubled, 300 to 600 kg per hectare. Recent development of GM cotton has further increased the production by leaps and bounds. In 2002, GM cotton accounted for almost 30 per cent of global cotton production; USA more than 70 per cent, followed by Australia 40 per cent, China 20 per cent while in India it is about 1 per cent.

Cotton marketing is the interaction of cotton farmers, traders (cotton ginning and pressing) and cotton textile mills. When cotton arrives in the market from October onwards in large quantity, the prices in the market fall sometimes below MSP. With arrival of cotton in the market from October to February the price of cotton decreases or rises very marginally and from March onwards price starts picking up and is at its pick in September. The average difference between price is as high as Rs.1350 per quintal. Since the holding capacity of the farmer is very limited he sells cotton in distress. Sometimes, farmer stands in a queue in the cotton market for four to five days to sell his cotton. He is at the mercy of the trader or government purchase agency. Those who purchase during this period (October to January) and sell later stand to gain.

Working textile mills numbering 1392 do not purchase cotton directly from the farmers, except a few who have contract farming arrangements with cotton farmers, as direct purchase by mills is not allowed under APMA and regulated markets. Average monthly cotton consumption by mills is more or less uniform between 11 to 12 lakhs bales. Mills, therefore, instead of purchasing cotton from farmers, processing and stocking and locking of finances, prefer to take supplies from CCI and private traders as and when they need it. CCI as a government agency purchases cotton at MSP when market price falls below the MSP and supplies cotton to mills at clean profit of crore of rupees; Rs. 3.09 cro. after tax and interest in 2002-03. In fact, this profit should have gone to cotton farmers. The cotton farmers suffer worst when production exceeds demand and stocks pile up. This is increasingly going to be the scenario when productivity of cotton will increase adding to production exceeding the consumption.

Farmers produce superior (25 cm to 27 cm), long staple (27 to 32 cm) and extra long (32 cm and above) in large quantity. In 2001-02, out of total production of 158 lakh bales (bale=170 kg), 110 lakh bales were of superior, long and extra long staple quality. It is therefore not correct to say that Indian cotton is of inferior quality. It is quite competitive against the imported cotton. India is competing in the cotton textile market in world with use of local cotton and not imported cotton. What is lacking is the proper marketing arrangement of cotton that will benefit the farmers. There is 55 member Cotton Advisory Board (CAB) under the Ministry of Textiles originally set up in October 1958 and now reconstituted in February 2004. CAB advises government on matters relating to production, consumption and marketing of cotton and also provides a forum for liaison between Cotton Textile Mill Industry, the cotton growers, the cotton traders and the governments. In spite of such a largely represented body, the main problem of remunerative prices for cotton and proper supply and demand management to benefit the cotton farmers has not been evolved.

Another equally important aspect is low yields of cotton and fall in the area cultivated. In 2002-03 area under cultivation fell to 7.46 million hectare compared to 9.34 million hectare in 1998-99. The yield in 2002-03 deceased to 212 kg per hectare compared the highest yield achieved at 265 kg per hectare in 1996-97. There has been a continuous decline in yield since 1996-97. It is a serious matter and productivity of cotton needs to be addressed urgently. Though four Technology Missions on Cotton (TMC) are working, the impact seems to be weak in improving yields. The fall in the area under cotton shows that farmers are moving away from cotton cultivation to other crops on account of price risk and uncertain market condition. It is unique situation that under falling yields and fall in area under cultivation, there was glut in the market leading to fall in cotton prices affecting the income of the farmers adversely.

The ECA is being amended and cotton along with other commodities will be knocked off the essential commodities list.

Cotton will be further exposed to market forces. In a situation of glut in cotton market, the prices may become adverse to farmers. The decontrol of cotton may not need fixing MSP for cotton. In that case, previous years prices in the open market will be the guiding factor. As the farmers are not organized and large number of farmers are marginal and small, they will be further exposed to exploitation by traders. CCI is marginal player in purchase of cotton and will not be able to save farmers from traders. In that case, the situation of farmers will further worsen.

In a market driven era in agri-produce the cotton farmers who are already moving away from cotton cultivation may further accelerate this process. More cotton will be needed with abolition of quota in textile trade from 2005 under WTO. India has great opportunity to increase textile exports. In that case more cotton production is needed. Considering this development and to make the farmers better off, urgent steps are needed to get remunerative prices, establishing direct link between farmers with end users *i.e.* textile mills and laying down a sustained export policy to make Indian cotton more competitive in the world market.

Contract Farming is going to be a long term solution for marketing of cotton. The assured market with private sector investment of cotton textile industry in cotton farms and farmers will stabilize the economic conditions of farmers. The price paid will have very little fluctuations. After experiencing the advantage of contract farming more farmers will opt for this mode of marketing cotton and getting an assured return. Ministry of Agriculture has already prepared model rules and regulations of contract farming to safeguard the farmers from exploitation.

Cotton Farmers Development and Management Council (CFDMC) would be required to bring together all the seven players, namely cotton farmers, ginners and stockists, traders, cotton seed processors, agencies who produce, handle or market cotton/cotton seeds and textile mills. There is need to have formal organization that brings seven players together in an integrated manner. There exists Cotton Advisory Board functioning under the Ministry of Textile but its thrust is in tackling the problem of cotton farmers and making him integral part of user industry is not significant. If it would have been very significant then farmers would not have landed in misery that led them to commit suicide. The important aspect of

CFDMC in the marketing of cotton would be to extend the cotton market to world wide on the pattern of National Cotton Council (NCC) of USA. NCC represents seven cotton segments as detailed above. It communicates United Industry positions on various agencies on various issues to approach government bodies and working for policy that assures world wide competitiveness and protects members income. NCC's value of cotton trade is $120 billion annually providing jobs to 3.40 lakh cotton farmers and millions in affiliated industries. In addition, Cotton US Program (CUSP) reaches about 3 billion current and potential customers in more than 50 countries. NCC of USA and CUSP pulls more cotton into marketing system that benefits the farmers and all downstream industries. It is on this pattern the CFDMC is to function integrating contract farming system into marketing of cotton nationally and internationally. Cotton Corporation of India (CCI) can also be revamped with the above functions instead of setting up new organization–CFDMC.

Using Cotton Staple Measuring Machines for payment of cotton is the immediate step to pay farmers for the cotton they bring to the market. Presently, the payment is based on large varieties of cotton that delays the payment. After all the superior or inferior variety of cotton is decided on the basis of staple count. The use of staple measuring machine will facilitate efficiency in marketing system and enhance confidence of the farmer and enable him to get the payment on the spot like that of the milk seller who is paid immediately on the basis of fat content of the milk. The drill for payment by using cotton staple machine can be started urgently to demonstrate farmers its utility in getting quick payment.

The most important factor that will benefit farmers is marketing arrangement for cotton that will fetch good price to him. The prosperity of cotton farmer of USA is dependent on export of cotton. Top customers of US cotton are Mexico (20 per cent), Turkey (12 per cent), Indonesia (11 per cent), and China (9 per cent). If US cotton can be sold to far distant customers like Indonesia and China why Indian cotton can not be sold to these countries who are geographically near to us giving advantage in transport cost.

GM Cotton Intensification Program in India needs to be introduced given the modest growth in consumption and poor price prospects. Reducing cost of production through GM cotton is imperative for cotton dependent countries. China adopted 11 GM varieties and with that the major benefits went to farmers (small holders) mainly because of use of public funds. In other cotton producing countries the benefits due to private funds went to biotech and seed companies. The program in India of GM cotton should result in benefits to small farmers and not to biotech and seed companies.

International Promotion of Indian Cotton should be undertaken to help farmers in earning higher income. Recently an initiative has been undertaken by the International Cotton Advisory Committee to establish international cotton promotion program.

The International Forum for Cotton Promotion (IFCP) was established in 2003. The objective of the Forum is to encourage and facilitate national market development programs, organized by associations and commercial organizations in individual countries and funded from domestic resources. Forum is supposed to be clearing house for exchange of proven ideas and strategies to be implemented by national organization. The Cotton Advisory Board can develop such a Forum as a link to IFCP to promote Indian cotton overseas.

Farmer Centric Marketing Organizations: Unite for Profits

The farmers in India are not organized to push reforms that are needed for better prices for their produce, demand supply management and protective umbrella in times of emergency. As the data given in the foregoing pages shows, large number of farmers are marginal and small and hardly have any impact on the market. In addition they are geographically scattered. Only thing that can bring them together and identify themselves is commodity he produces. The cotton or sugarcane producing farmers, though scattered geographically can come together under one flag of their produce as it is that which gives them their income. Not much attention has been paid to this gravitating force of commodity pull to unite them for profit.

In developed countries farmers have got organized under the banner of the commodity that they produce. Farmers producing pulses are organized, titled UNIGRAINS, that decides about production and marketing of pulses for better prices and links itself with users of pulses. It communicates with the government on important policies relating to prices etc. It disseminates information to all the pulses growers on market trends. Plain Cotton Cooperative Association (PCCA) of USA is another cotton farmers' organization that markets 2.5 to 3 million bales annually. It was founded in 1953 by group of visionary farmers to get best possible prices. It is the largest farmer owned organization in the world.

Once the agri-produce is exposed to open market, not much help from government is expected and farmers will have to set up organizations owned by them for specific commodity. What the government can do in the intervening period is to bring together enlightened and visionary farmers to form farmer-owned organization for specific commodities or group of commodities. Agriculture marketing experts can assist such a group of farmers. In the initial stages leaders of farmers from developed countries who have set up such organizations can help setting up farmers' organization. As an experiment in this field, farmer leaders can be given contract to set up commodity specific organization on turn key basis. Government role is going to be abridged in open market situation and farmers will have to find solution to problems of marketing and pricing of their products.

New NGOs who can work for organizing farmers commodity-wise on the pattern of developed countries should be given encouragement or the existing NGOs who have good linkages with farmers can start this work. As an initiative, government may set up a Committee which will give an operational blue print or Group of NGOs may set up working group to give guidance to farmers to bring home the message of "uniting for profit" to the farmers. Common economic interest of farmers of specific commodity can bring them together.

Chapter 6

Farmers' Income, Rural and Social Transformation (FIRST): Income Kit for Farmers

The income policy for the farmers in India does not exist per se. As has been described in the foregoing Chapters, the income of the farmers is declining and it has become necessary to plan for sustained increase in their income especially when domestic demand for their produce is sluggish. This is adversely affecting the farm economy of India as farmers and agriculture labour are opting for the exit route to urban areas or committing suicide. The farm sector is becoming unpopular occupation as revealed by the situation assessment of farmers in the NSSO 59th Round. The income policy for the farmers was not thought so far as the market forces yielded adequate income to the farmers in a situation of scarcity of food grains and other cash crops as also subsidies on input. But the opening of the economy under the WTO Regime and liberalization in the domestic economy the input costs have increased with the reduction in subsidies and due to surplus in production vis-à-vis current demand, the prices of agriculture produce declined or remained static during the last five years.

This resulted in fall in prices and in some cases farmers are not being paid in full leading to large payment arrears. Due to paucity of financial resources, the government intervention to purchase the surplus production led to the fall in the open market prices much below the Minimum Support Prices. The overall impact was the fall in the real income of the farmers at the macro-level as stated in Chapter I. The income generated in the agriculture sector in absolute and proportional terms is not keeping pace with burden of population in this sector. India can not opt for de-population of agriculture sector unlike the developed countries as the urban sector is bursting to its seams. Urban sector can not absorb increased influx of rural unemployed even at the current pace. How then to provide adequate income to the farmers that will not only sustain them but also to gear up the rural economy for increased circulation of income to farmers. And this is to be achieved within the structure of existing small farms as this can not be tinkered beyond certain limit without the consent of the farmer. The Income Policy for the farmers in India is to be then evolved by bringing in sources of income to the farm gates and arranging to give them remunerative prices for their produce. It is in this context that the income and employment generation at the farm gate is imperative.

Farmers' Income Policy of Developed Countries

The developed countries also faced fall in income of their farmers during the course of their economic journey in the past. In the United States, the income policy took roots in 1936. It meant Parity of Incomes (PI) in the rural and urban areas. PI meant income necessary to maintain ratio between the purchasing power of the net income per person on farms and that of non-farm that prevailed over five year period *i.e.* August 1909 to August 1914. It related to the gross family income necessary to guarantee the standard of living in farm household equal to persons dependent on other occupations. Incomes policy in this sense was to aim at minimizing difference in income of the farmers and those engaged in other non-farm activities. It is a means to keep the farming an equally popular occupation. The objectives of the income policy were stable price ratios of farm products fixed at some historical period, achieve goal of parity income *i.e.* equal level of incomes and equal standard of living for farmers and non-farmers. These objectives of income policy were achieved by combination of policy instruments such as shifting rural farm population to urban areas in non-farm occupations, investment in rural areas reducing gaps in urban and rural infrastructure in transport and communications and other amenities. Most importantly price support system was put in position, land use planning to manage supply-demand balance and subsidizing export of farm products to dispose of surplus production and finally to compensate farmers through direct money payments to maintain parity incomes and standard of living. The farmer population in USA is about 1.5 per cent of total population and agri-GDP is only about 2 per cent of total GDP.

Similarly, developed countries of European Union have Common Agriculture Policy (CAP) which contains important component of income policy for farmers. CAP was initiated in 1962 and continues to be modified from time to time to accommodate the changing economic environment in EU countries. CAP is based on three major principles namely unified market with free flow of agriculture commodities, product preference in internal market over imports through customs tariffs and common financing of agriculture programs. Under the CAP the main objectives are to increase agriculture production, ensure fair standard of living for farmers, stabilize market, guarantee regular food supplies and ensure reasonable prices to consumers. For protecting and increasing farmers' income, the main instruments of incomes policy are price support, direct payments to farmers, supply control and border measures.

The income policy is operated through Common Organizations of Agriculture Markets (COM) which exist for most EU agriculture products. They eliminate obstacles to the intra-union trade of agriculture products and main customs barriers. COMs are extended to all products excepting potatoes and spirits. COMs are involved in large market interventions and budget costs (grains, beef, dairy and oilseeds). It is the biggest public intervention for market mechanism. Intervention mechanism ensured a guaranteed outlet for quantities produced. There is EU agriculture budget to safe guard farmers' income and take care of rural infrastructure. It is managed by European Agriculture Guidance and Guarantee Fund (EAGGF). The Guidance Section contributes to structural reforms and development of rural areas and promotes rural development. Guarantee Section provides funds for expenditure concerning the cost to buy, store surplus production and encourage agriculture exports. When the agriculture production in EU led to surplus in number of products resulting in sharp fall in open market prices, Domestic Price Support (DPS) mechanism of price intervention and high tariffs was evolved. DPS is market intervention to buy supplies when the prices threaten to fall below agreed minimum (intervention) prices. Through DPS unlimited excess products are purchased that can not be sold in open market. Surplus items are stored in EU's storage facilities and exported with subsidies. This protects farmers' income on a sustained basis besides the direct payments made to them to provide improved standard of living. For fruits and vegetables Authorised Producers Organizations (APO) are allowed to withdraw supplies in limited quantities from the market when market prices fall below specified levels. The emphasis of the income policy has shifted from price support to income support policy since 1990 though commodity support prices continue, but at lower levels. The sustained increase in farmers' income is the main objective of EU countries along with the maintaining of small farms, avoid congestion in the cities and eradicating the food scarcity. CAP is continued in the EU with its 25 Members now for the benefit of the farmers though it imposes costs on consumers through extra food prices.

Any Income Policy for Indian Farmers ?

So far there is no well laid out Income Policy for farmers to ensure sustained increase in their income as would be revealed from the previous Chapters. India has explicit agriculture policy to achieve self sufficiency in food grains and other agriculture produce by increasing land under irrigation and providing agriculture inputs such as seeds, insecticides, fertilizer and other inputs at subsidized rates. The marketing of agriculture products is arranged in regulated markets under APMA of the respective State governments. In the transition phase of scarcity of food grains and cash crops such as cotton, sugarcane and jute, the farmers received remunerative prices for their products in the open market. When the surpluses arose in food grains production the prices started decreasing. In order to avoid food scarcity and encouraging the farmers to retain land for food grains production and also to give support to farmers that will cover their cost of production and to build adequate stock of food grains, government evolved mechanism of Minimum Support Prices (MSP) for selected 25 commodities. To protect the farmers' income from falling especially of food grains government entered in the market to purchase food grains at MSP and ensured food safety. MSP is a mechanism to cover the cost of production incurred by farmers. It does not provide any additional income even for his managerial services. MSP is the cost related subsistence price. The details about the MSP fixation has been elaborated in Chapter IV.

The pitiable condition of cotton and sugarcane farmers in a situation of surpluses under monopoly cotton purchase by the government and under agreed sugarcane supplies to sugar mills has been highlighted in Chapter IV.

There is hardly any well-knit thinking on sustained increase in farmers' income in the government nor there are farmers' organization that will take care of their income. The old arrangement of APMA for marketing of agri-produce is resulting in increased costs to him and low prices. Essential Commodities Act is hampering free movement of agri-products. Government financial resources are falling short of required purchases of surplus production especially of food grains at MSP from all the areas to give relief to farmers. The private sector initiative for marketing of agri-produce is still at the showcase level and Commodity Exchanges set up for information to farmers about the prices prevailing at different places are at infancy stage.

Given the small size of the villages and farms, low level of education and awareness of the farmers as revealed by the NSSO 59th Round and obstacles in the accessibility, majority of the farmers fail to take advantage of these developments. In a federal set up of governance, agriculture is a State subject and hence limitation of formulating a Unified Incomes Policy (UIP) for farmers. The government's policies, programs and research continue to focus on increase in agriculture production and not on the farmers' income primarily. There is a talk to double the food grains production from 200 million tonnes to 400 million tonnes but not much attention to double the farmers' income from the present level in a given time frame. Farmers' income is implicitly considered to be the fall out of increased production. But that is not the case as revealed by the income crisis of the farm community in India in the recent past. Time has come to lay down an explicit Unified Income Policy for Farmers (UIPF) to ensure sustained increase in their income.

The analysis in the foregoing Chapters has established the fact that a specific and well focussed policy for increase in farmers' income is imperative. General agricultural growth does not seem to be an answer for sustained increase in farmers' income. Much needs to be done to design income policy that will suit Indian farm sector keeping in view the limitations of resources and still making best use of the resources by internalising the gains of agricultural growth and market development for raising farmers' income on a sustained basis.

It is with this consideration that Farmers' Income, Rural and Social Transformation (FIRST) has been designed to lay down the basics of operational design of Farmers' Income Policy.

While the macro level policy and schemes and program to increase agriculture production and productivity do have positive effect but the filtering of such benefits becomes weak for marginal and small farmers. This is mainly due to costs of marketing, virtually no margin of profit in MSP, open market prices sometimes being less than MSP and inadequate support of procurement by public agencies. In case of surplus production the farmer is the sufferer as seen during the last five years. Due to liberalization of trade and reduction in input subsidies, farmer's income has been declining. It is in this context that for marginal and small farmers a sustainable income kit needs to be designed. There are two aspects to this design: first is the per capita Agri-GDP of the States and the commodity specific measures that will benefit the farmers directly.

Pyramid of Income Levels of States

The average per capita Agri-GDP at all India level is Rs.4608 in 2001-02. Based on this, States are classified in two categories. The State-wise per capita GDP is given in Table 4 in Chapter I.

Table 11: Classification of States by Level of Per Capita Agri-GDP

Category	*States*
A. Above	
All India Av.	Punjab, Haryana, Karnatak, Goa, Mizoram, Nagaland, Maharashtra, Gujarat, Tamilnadu, J & K, Andhra Pradesh, Tripura (12)
B. Below	
All India Av.	Kerala, West Bengal, Madhya Pradesh, Himachal Pradesh, Arunachal Pradesh, Rajasthan, Uttar Pradesh, Meghalaya, Sikkim, Orissa, Assam, Manipur, Bihar (13)

Of the 25 States, Category A States have per capita Agri-GDP above national average indicating that at the macro level the Green Revolution package seems to have increased Agri-GDP reasonably well to generate income for the farmers and rural population. In Category B States the Green Revolution package and other programs have not been very effective to raise Agri-GDP which is reflected in lower levels of income of the farmers and high pressure of rural population. In designing income kit for the farmers, precedence will have to be given to farmers in Category B States so that in the first place they catch up with the all India average per capita GDP of 2001-02 and move further on the pyramid. However, even in the Category A States, commodity specific problems are faced by the farmers that reduces their income. The case in point is the Cotton and Sugarcane farmers of Maharashtra, A.P. and UP who faced the problem of falling incomes leading to suicide. The above classification is useful to policy makers at the Central and State level to design schemes and programs that will increase Agri-GDP on a priority basis and make provision of financial resources. The major emphasis has to be commodity specific income kit for the farmers across the States.

Commodity and Non-Commodity Dimensions

The farmer's income in general and marginal and small farmers' income in particular is influenced by commodity and non-commodity developments and changes in rural areas. The main source of farmer's income is size of his produce and the price that he receives for the produce. Increase in production and or increase in price fetches more income to the farmer. This can increase income upto a point as the production finally is constrained by the size of land that he cultivates. The size, given the ownership pattern, can not be increased and with more pressure of population on land it is further fragmented and size of land further decreases. Further increase in production through double cropping, using irrigation and high yielding seeds and improving fertility of the land can enhance the economic size of the land.

After this limit is reached income from land reaches a ceiling level for the farmers and further increase in income will have to come from non-land sources such as agro-forestry, on-farm fishing, agro-processing, non-farm employment and finally reducing number of persons in farmer's household *i.e.* migration. All such sources and other infrastructure developments including transport and communications that will help increase farmer's income can be grouped in non-commodity category. In fact direct positive impact on farmers' income comes by expanding the commodity dimension *i.e.* production on land and price that farmer receives for the produce. The non-commodity dimension has impact on income indirectly and comes up with time lag. The farmers, particularly marginal and small, have too much to do to just produce the crop and often does not have the marketing background to generate demand for produce or promote sales. Either the assistance has to come from government agency or farmers have to collectively engage in marketing activities and ask for more non-farm incomes by developing other economic activities. J.M Keynes, a great economic policy economist, while presenting his grand design at Bretonwoods Institutions in 1943 had suggested Commodity Control Organizations to safeguard the interest of the farmers. U.S.A. opposed it on the ground of free trade. In practice, however, EU with its Common Commodity Organizations is practicing Keynes's CCO to protect farmers' income. Therefore, commodity dimension has been presented in farmer centric income kit.

The commodity-farmer centric income kit is essential for the sheer number of farmers whose income is to be protected and increased. There are 178.3 million farmers cultivating 147.89 million hectare. Out of this, rice and wheat farmers are 86 million (51 per cent) and if 35.54 million farmers producing coarse grains are included the total number of farmers producing cereals touches a staggering figure of 121.98 million (75 per cent). There are 69 million marginal and small farmers producing rice and wheat. What prices they get for their produce and what income they get is the most important issue of income policy.

Commodity-Farmer Centric Income Generating Kit

While formulating schemes and programs for farmers the main emphasis has always been on increasing production and productivity and it is implicitly taken for granted that farmers' income will increase as a fall out effect. In the initial stages of scarcity of agriculture produce, the farmers got better prices and incomes increased. But since late 1990s and with trade liberalization and storage based food security, prices increased by small margins. By end 1990s and during the last five years with surpluses of agri-produce and procurement confined to rice and wheat, the farm prices fell affecting the farmer's income adversely. The macro level changes in marketing reforms and price discovery in agri-produce and Commodity Exchanges are progressing but rather slowly. Direct positive impact on farmer's income is hardly perceptible making agriculture an unpopular profession as brought out by the 59th Round of NSSO. In fact, the farmers will have to be more organized to demand their share of income if it does not flow from macro level policies and programs. In view of this commodity-farmer centric price and non-price support is needed to add to farmer's income directly. Price and non-price support measures to increase farmer's income by commodities are given in Annexure V.

The major contents of income kit of the farmers are the commodity pricing and supply demand management and support from government and other agencies in times of excess production. The short term and the long term price and non-price support measures have been spelt out by commodities as general marketing reforms do not have the thrust that is needed at the commodity level. It will be for the farmers and their organizations to take up steps for its implementation. CACP goes in depth at the commodity level problems while determining the MSP/SMP. CACP Reports are very rarely used in taking steps to improve farmers' income. MSP/SMP fixation only receives government attention. CACP Reports have been used intensively in preparing commodity specific income kits for the farmers. The developed countries who were confronted with the declining income of the farmers in mid 1980s had taken commodity specific price and non-price measures to bring about sustained increase in farmers' income. It is hoped that Indian farmers and their organizations at the all India and local level will take commodity centric price and non-price support measures to improve income as detailed in Annexure V.

In EU under Commodity Market Organizations and under the overall umbrella of Common Agricultural Policy (CAP), farmer's income is protected through support prices and intervention procurements and stocking and exporting overseas. Heavy subsidization is done for this purpose. In USA commodity Boards or Councils managed by farmers and assisted by government safeguard farmers' income. American Soyabean Association illustrates how farmers' Commodity Organization can make farmers rich. The self-help of the farmers and extension services of the agricultural institution can help in safeguarding and increasing farmer's income. Farmers require lot of promotional efforts from extension agencies and experts to organizing themselves as they lack skills to market their produce. But once the promotional support is provided farmers are fast learners and they can contribute a lot to improve their income. An illustrious case is Sonoma County located 50 miles from San Francisco, California, USA. The following Box gives in nutshell how farmers' organization can play wonders if they get promotional assistance from extension, agriculture experts and marketers.

Sonoma County Farmers
(Sonoma, 50 miles from San Francisco, California, USA)

Sonoma County Select seal

1. Farmers produced grapes, fruits, dairy, meat and speciality foods of the area. They faced difficulties due to increasing competition from out-of the State marketing program, foreign products and urbanization pressure. The income of the farmers was falling.
2. Sonoma County Agriculture Marketing Program (SCAMP) was prepared by the Cooperative extension Services of the University of California. In 1987 Extension Staff contacted the interactive farmers, processors and marketers to promote local agri-produce and services.
3. County Board of Supervisors appointed 21 Member Blue Ribbon Task Force which included marketing and agriculture experts. The Group Empowerment program started under this umbrella organization.
4. County-wide marketing through media contacts, marketing logo, food fairs and educational programs for producers, buyers and consumers were taken up. Logo (shown above) gave identity for local produce and quality and helped in promoting sales, opening distribution channels and reaching large number of consumers. Business friendship was developed based on cooperation and shared interests.
5. Economic Development Board provided initial seed capital.
6. By 1989 the Membership increased from 18 to 270 consisting of growers, processors and marketers. This enabled the farmers to increase income and stay in agriculture in the face of urban pressure and competition.

Source: Journal of Extension. Fall 1992. Vol.30. No.3. University of California, USA.

The start up funding support was provided in the form of seed money of $25,000 by Sonoma County Economic Development Board. The grant of $75,000 came from County Board of Supervisors and another $58,000 as promotional funding from the County. That stabilized the SCAMP financially and that made positive impact on farmers' income. A farmer has summed up the effect in these words: "SCAMP has the potential to really help specific agricultural industries with its program in education, diversification, research and tourism." The Sonoma Model shows the way as to how commodity-farmer centric income generating kit can be developed in practice. In India, the extension efforts in agriculture so far concentrated on advising farmers to increase production and yield. Now the extension services are required to create consumer demand and organize marketing to increase farmers' income and create environment so that they stay in agriculture.

Non-Commodity Dimension

Commodity-farmer centric income kit has direct impact on increasing farmers' income based on direct price and non-price supports. This alone is not enough. This needs to be extended and made an integral part of marketing net work at the local, regional and national level for agriculture produce. The supply chain from farm gate to dinner table also provides scope and margin to get a better deal to the farmer to reduce his costs and increase income in the process. The non-commodity dimension *i.e.* marketing institutions and rural and social infrastructure are the next in chain to increase farmers' income and consolidate his position as pro-active partner in changing the rural economic landscape. Two areas in this context are A. Market Institutions and Integration, and B. Macro Investment Activity in Farm Sector.

A. Market Institutions and Integration

Spatial interactions of farmers with other agencies in the supply chains are determined in the market for his produce. These interactions may remain limited to local rural market when the marketable surplus is very small. It further extends to markets of small towns and further to processors, wholesalers and retailers till it reaches consumers' table. Spatial interaction is not limited to agriculture produce but to flow of people from rural to urban areas, money and information and banking services from urban to rural areas. They form important part of market integration of farmers. This non-commodity dimension *i.e.* market integration can help to reduce the cost of marketing to farmers and get better prices for their produce. The traditional supply chain has more intermediaries which adds to farmer's transportation and transaction costs compared to modern supply chain which reduces these intermediate market players. The Studies of FICCI and ADB have quantified these costs as already mentioned in Chapter I.

The Chapter on Marketing Reforms has highlighted the need to move from regulated markets to farmer friendly markets by dismantling restrictions on the movement of farmers' produce direct to processors and to final consumers. Adoption of Model APMA by the State government can reduce costs of marketing for the farmers and fetch more income to them. Since the regulated markets generate some revenue to the States they are either slow in implementing the Model APMA or may need more time. In order to expedite this process some compensation can be paid to them to reduce cost of marketing to farmers to add to their income.

Market integration is a process to bring farmers face to face with business and consumers. Farmers are often small producers of low-tech primary products and hardly involves processing in rural areas. This large fragmented group of farmers is to be integrated in the large gamut of marketing arrangement. Forming of producers organization *i.e.* Commodity Boards has already been detailed above. On the non-commodity dimension, three major areas need to be improved for market integration of farmers to reduce costs to the farmers and increase their income.

Reducing Transaction and Transportation Costs

Transaction costs can be considerably brought down by forming farmers groups and cooperatives and producers' marketing association to deal collectively with other players in the markets on the pattern of milk cooperatives, sugarcane farmers and vegetables marketed on a cooperative basis such as Mother Diary outlets in Delhi. Collective efforts of small producers can reduce their transaction costs, identifies the proper partners, increases bargaining power and capacity to bear risk and finally helps in reducing marketing costs. Bringing together farmers, retailers and consumers is an important institutional (non-commodity area) reform that will help farmers to reduce transactions costs and add to their income.

The transportation cost forms an important component of marketing costs especially for marginal and small farmers. Much depends upon the connectivity of rural areas by all weather roads that facilitates the movement of goods from rural to urban areas. In the non-commodity development having a bearing on costs to farmers rural road infrastructure is the most crucial area for better integration of rural farm activities to marketing in urban areas. Coming together of farmers in producers' groups and cooperatives can reduce individual costs and risks in marketing their produce. This is a very weak aspect of rural marketing. Not much has been done to organize marketing of agri-produce collectively.

Price Transferancy

Lack of information on open market prices of agri-produce often deprives farmers to get best prices for their produce. This happens due to the lack of information to farmers on prevailing prices in other marketing centres. Small and scattered farmers need an organized institutional arrangement which will help them to sell their commodities at best of prices. Since it is difficult for farmers to discover best prices for their produce, farm commodity exchanges have been set up recently in the private sector. They make information available on-line for the benefit of the farmers and even arrange delivery of the items. Considering the limitations of farmers to access this information many private corporate sector companies have set up Price Discovery Kiosks known as e Chaupals (common meeting place of farmers in village) that brings price information at the door steps of the farmers. The private sector efforts in this direction have been elaborated in Chapter IV. It has helped farmers to get farm inputs from low cost destination and selling their items at high price destinations. e Chaupals as price discovery centres need to be enlarged and coverage expanded. Added to this is an institutional arrangement to make every village a Knowledge Centre that is also catching up which provides more information on other aspects of production, productivity and marketing to the farmers.

Policy Related Barriers

The policy related barriers can have adverse effect on farmers' income. A set of policy measures adopted in a scarcity situation may become unsuitable when surplus arises in the market. The regulated markets under APMA and Essential Commodities Act served the farmers and consumers well at the time of food scarcity but now in a situation of surplus of agri-produce these policy instruments have become barriers in reducing costs to farmers and increasing income. Restriction on inter-State movement of food grains restrict the farmers to get the prices available. Public sector monopoly in procurement of food grains is increasing the cost of storage. More private sector participation can help farmers and business. Government has already taken steps to dismantle these policy related barriers for the benefit of the farmers. Farmers and industry have to adjust to these changes. Sugar industry has now been decontrolled and with surplus sugar production vis-à-vis demand the price of sugar declined during the last three years. This resulted in delayed payment to sugarcane farmers. With the removal of policy barriers new supply-demand matrix will have to be evolved so that farmers and industry benefit collectively. A new ethos of production and marketing will have to be in place when the policy barriers are dismantled as is now happening in India. This non-commodity dimension is going to play crucial role in time to come.

B. Macro Investment Activity in Farm Sector

The macro investment activity such as irrigation schemes, land development, provision of working capital *i.e.* through banking channel and roads and communication has trickle down effect on farmers productivity and on income. It builds a sound economic base to sustain agriculture activities that benefits marginal and small farmers in particular. These investment activities have a spread and spin off effect for the development of rural sector of which agriculture sector is the major beneficiary. The infrastructure up-gradation is key to increase the size of agri-GDP and increase per capita agri-GDP of farmers. Gross Fixed Capital Formation (GFCF) is an indicator of the level of macro investment activity in farm sector.

GFCF in public sector includes irrigation projects undertaken by government agencies. The private sector GFCF consists of investment by corporate sector in plantation activities in Tea, Coffee, Rubber etc. In the household sector, the activities relating to construction of bunds, digging of wells and similar activities are included in Agri-GFCF. The Agri-GFCF as percentage of GDP decreased from 1.92 per cent in1990-91 to 1.31 in 2003-04. The share of private sector GFCF in total GFCF increased from 70.4 per cent to 74.4 per cent during this period but public sector share fell from 29.6

per cent to 25.6 per cent. It may be pointed out that private sector GFCF is limited to plantation sector and does not contribute to rest of the agriculture sector.

With the fall in public sector GFCF, the capacity of the agriculture sector is bound to dwindle. This shows the less attention paid to agriculture sector during the last decade and half. Hence there is urgent need to cover this backlog of GFCF in agriculture and boost it further. Most of the State governments have huge debt burden and hence less public investment in agriculture. Looking to the financial health of the State Governments and even a State like Maharashtra reeling under huge debt of Rs.1.10 lakh crores, huge investment in farm sector is imperative.

Irrigation is key to enhance agriculture production and makes it possible to diversify to other crops. It also helps in adding fertilizers to increase the yield. The prosperity of Punjab and Haryana farmers is mainly dependent on efficient and wide spread irrigation net work. Added to this is the connectivity by roads to urban areas. If the farmers are to be benefited, then a whole scheme of this kind of non-commodity investment by public and private sector is needed. Those States which are at the bottom of the per capita Agri-GDP need to be given priority in strengthening GFCF. The water harvesting schemes in dry farming areas also have to get precedence for benefiting the farmers directly. Farmers in fact may not require waiving of electricity charges or interest rate payment but want all those input which will increase production and get better prices with increase in rural based economic activities.

In-Sourcing Farm Activities

New agro based economic activities can be in-sourced for the farmers. Cluster of villages can be selected by private and public agencies to carry out gradation and sorting of farm commodities and wherever possible do some semi processing especially in fruits and vegetables rather than taking up these activities in urban centres. Such an in-sourcing is not difficult. It needs organizational efforts and some tax incentives and concessions to private sector to initiate such activities. Radial Agro-Processing expounded in Chapter IV can be a big in-sourcing for increase in income and employment. Large storage centres can be built in cluster of villages rather than building big silos in urban areas. This will save cost of transport to urban areas and bring the same produce back for consumption in rural areas. Public Distribution of food grains and other items of mass consumption can be in-sourced to rural sector which should generate economic activities for farmers and rural people.

Out-Sourcing Forests to Farmers

There are new areas which need to be tapped for the benefit of the farmers wherever it is possible with initial technical and financial support to farmers. One such area is Agro-forestry Plantation. With the signing of Kyoto Protocol by 141 countries in February 2005 voluntary carbon offset market is growing fast Selling certified Tradable Carbon Offsets (CTOs) is developing a big business. In simple terms it is taking up local forestry on behalf of the developed countries. According to Kyoto Protocol developed countries have to reduce their GHG emission by an average of 5.2 per cent below their 1990 level by 2020. To meet this target, the developed countries are farming out forest development in developing countries. This out-sourcing of forest by developed countries can be good source of income to farmers.

Some initiatives have been taken by the farmers and their organizations. About 50 Indian projects with potential to generate 300 million tonnes of Certified Emission Reduction (CER) over a period of 10 years are in the stage of project formulation and finalization stage. They are to be registered at UN Framework Convention on Climate Change (UNFCCC) by December 2005. The Indian projects may get affected if deadline is not met or is not extended. Each CER stands for one tonne of carbon dioxide reduction and can be traded globally.

Friends of Carbon (FoC), a Pune based (Maharashtra) NGO, has already brought together 5000 farmers to exploit the option which permits the developed countries to meet part of the targeted emission cuts by funding tree plantations in developing countries. Farmers need a minimum 50,000 acres to begin trade in Carbon Credit. This scheme can be a bonus to old plantation owners. They can earn enough carbon credits trading. 90 per cent of funds earned by FoC will go to farmers, 5 per cent to its associates and 5 per cent to pay to International Finance Corporation (IFC) which will act as a mediator and facilitate interaction with developed countries like Japan and Europe.

Madhya Pradesh government sponsored cultivation of Jatropa trees. It has picked up and is helping to earn additional income to the farmers. The State government vehicles are being run on the oil derived from Jaropa and is receiving good support from other organizations. These and similar produce have to be out-sourced to farmers so that marginal and small farmers' income can supplement the income from cultivation.

BOT Strategy for Farmers

It is an acknowledged fact that leakages of public delivery system are big and it is difficult to check them in a corrupt administration set up. It is already known that in a rupee only 20 paise reaches the beneficiaries. This is true for rural and urban areas. Off late government and public agencies have started contracting to private sector to provide various goods and services in a time frame ensuring an agreed quality. In urban areas construction of roads, distribution of electricity, managing tolls and similar items are being given on contract on the principal of " Build, Operate and Transfer (BOT)". This has ensured timely completion and ensuring of quality, improving the delivery system and plugging leakage of public funds. Private sector participation in railways is being encouraged to improve services. Even the defence sector has opened its gates for private sector for this purpose.

The rural economic infrastructure and social transformation can be done on a contract basis under the BOT. Instead of scheme approach, project approach will be required for BOT strategy. The major beneficiaries will be farmers as they are the prime movers of economic development. Irrigation projects, roads, electricity installations, marketing yards, communication facilities and market information outlets can be contracted to private sector, cooperatives and NGO on BOT principle. The association of local farmers for prioritisation of projects on BOT basis should be the main ingredient in sanctioning such projects. Such projects will provide employment to local unemployed youths. They will get trained in private sector work culture and acquire skills. Government funds instead of going to government department should be given to private or contracted party based on the stages of completion of the project in a given time frame ensuring the agreed quality. The role of government should be largely promotional and monitoring the projects. The media is to be associated to report on the successes of BOT in rural areas and benefits derived by the rural people. The transfer of the projects and maintenance needs to be done by the local government with active association and participation of the rural people. The dependence on government is to be reduced increasingly for strengthening non-commodity area to increase farmers' income. In this process farmers will get activated and there will be more sense of participation rather than mere passive observers.

Income Boxes for Farmers

The above analysis opens two Income Boxes for farmers. They are Commodity and Non-Commodity Boxes. The Commodity Box directly adds to their income (Annexure V) while Non-Commodity Box improves the marketing institutions and integration and rural infrastructure to facilitate production and make rural area liveable place. In-sourcing economic activities is the key to farmers' income and employment. The following figure illustrates this new strategy.

Income Boxes of Farmers

Green Box *Commodity Box* *Direct Increase in Income*	*Amber Box* *Non-Commodity Box* *Indirect and delayed Increase in Income*
Price Support	Reform Market Institutions
Non-Price Support	Market Integration with Urban Areas
Committed Procurement	Reducing Transaction costs
Advance Price Signal	Price Transferancy
Eliminate Multiple-State Prices	Removal of Policy Barriers
No Payment Arrears	BOT for Economic Infrastructure
Commodity Organizations	Activating Farmers' Projects Selection
Except finances for procurement, other measures are non-resource using. Hence quick implementation for sustained increase in income.	The coverage will be more in this scheme with the existing resources by eliminating leakages and corruption and timely completion of projects. This accelerates increase in income.

The income boxes for the farmers is a mechanism that gives priority to farmers' income. Farmer is well versed in agriculture practice and there are very many institutions and organizations to assist him in increasing production and productivity. There is virtually no organization that monitors farmer's income on a regular basis. Fall in farmers income is dealt with in an ad hoc manner by announcing some relief such as waiving electricity bills, rescheduling debt and interest payments or some insurance scheme about which most farmers are not aware as revealed by the NSSO 59th round. What is needed is permanent set up in the Central and State governments that will monitor Framers' income index on a sustained basis. Such indices will have to be combination of macro and micro level indices so that timely and appropriate steps are taken to rejuvenate farmers' income.

Indexing Farmers' Income

The increase in agriculture production and food grains in particular was monitored by the government and necessary support of inputs and credit was made available to farmers for this purpose. But farmers' income has neither been indexed nor monitored. It seems that it was considered that increase in agriculture production and productivity will ipso facto increase farmers' income. But this is not happening off late when the surpluses have come up in the market and farmers are caught in the bind of low prices for their products and increase in cost of cultivation besides the sub-optimal size of land of marginal and small farmers. In order to correct this situation direct and indirect measures to increase farmers' income have been detailed above. But it will not be effective unless the farmers' income is indexed and these indices are monitored on a regular basis to take corrective steps to increase farmers' income on a sustained basis. For this purpose macro and micro indices of farmers income are presented below. They are in the nature of illustration and as a methodology. It is for the government to go into details and build such series like that of the whole sale price index or consumer price index.

Macro Indexing

National Agri-GDP Income Index

This index will measure the size of agriculture cake that is available to farmers and rural people. It is after all the size of the Agri-GDP which will show potential that has been realized in this sector. If the real Agri-GDP is static or there is meagre increase it means that with the heavy burden of population the per capita agri-GDP is decreasing and farmers' economic condition is worsening.

This has happened during the last three years. Table 12 illustrates Agri-GDP (1993-94 prices) Income Index.

Table 12: Agri-GDP Income Index (1993-94 Prices)
1998-99 = 100

Year	*GDP at Factor Cost from Agriculture (Rs. Crores)*	*Index*
1998-99	263540	100.0
1999-00	263258	99.8
2000-01	262196	99.4
2001-02	279871	106.2
2002-03	263096	99.8
2003-04	NA	
2004-05	NA	

The above Index shows that real GDP from agriculture is stagnating at 1998-99 level except for 2000-01. The increase in 2001-02 is also the previous year's low base. The base year of the Index can be decided by the Statistical office. This is the first Index at the national level that needs to be monitored at the National and State level as this will give signal about the farmers' economic position. If the real agri-GDP has stagnated almost for last five years it is loud call that farmers' income is bound to go down given the heavy pressure of population. This will be reflected in Per Capita Agri-GDP Index.

Per Capita Agri-GDP Index

From the national level of Agri-GDP, per capita Agri-GDP can be worked out, which will give information about average income level of farmer.

The above index at the national level shows that economic condition of farmers and rural people is worsening. Similar index worked out for States will give information about the economic situation of farmers in those States. The per capita Agri-GDP of the States for the year 2000-01 given in Table 4 in Chapter I can be taken as the base year and index for the subsequent years can be prepared.

The Per capita Agri-GDP Indices would be useful to the Central and State governments at the macro level to monitor the incomes of the farmers and rural people and take action in time to boost Agri-GDP. Such Indices can be compiled at the State level to identify where the income situation is worsening and where it is stagnant or improving. The refining in these Indices can be done by the government agencies as they have the accurate information available to them. Such Indices will be acceptable if they are compiled and released by government on a regular basis.

Agri-Commodity Income Index

The Income Indices will be more useful if they can be compiled at the commodity level for the farmers. The Indices can be compiled on the basis of yield per hectare and the MSP that the farmer is supposed to get. MSP-based income per hectare will be the Index of the income of marginal farmer. That is the lowest level of income that the farmer will get. It is illustrated for Rice and Wheat.

Table 13: Agri-Commodity Income Index (2000-01=100)

Yield: Quintal/per hectare
MSP: Rs. per quintal

Year	*Rice*				*Wheat*			
	Yield	*MSP*	*Income Per Hectare*	***Index***	*Yield*	*MSP*	*Income Per Hectare*	***Index***
2000-01	19.61	510	10,001	100	27.08	610	12,859	100
2001-02	20.79	530	11,018	110	27.62	620	17,400	135
2002-03	17.89	550	9,839	98	26.17	630	16,487	128
2003-04	19.00	550	10,550	104	27.50	630	17,325	135
2004-05	20.00	560	11,200	112	28.00	640	17,920	139

The above Index indicates about the changes in farmer's income level at the MSP for one acre land. This is the lowest income that he gets which covers his cost of cultivation as MSP only covers cost of cultivation (C2 cost). Farmer's yield is crucial to increase his income and if the open market price falls below MSP and there is no procurement to support him, farmer's income will further fall. This Index would alert the government agency about the steps which should be taken to protect the marginal and small farmers. Such Commodity Indices can be compiled for other commodities at the all India and State level. This will also show the sub-optimal size of land and need to increase its economic size increasing the intensity of cultivation and other non-farm and off-farm sources that will increase his income. The compilation of Income Indices will have to be taken up by a government on the pattern of WPI, CPI, Industrial Production Index etc. Such a quantitative index is needed if farmer's economic situation is to be monitored.

Income Targeting and Monitoring

The agriculture break through during the Green Revolution strategy was achieved by setting the targets of agriculture production within a given time frame. On similar lines the target for increase in farmers' income in a given time frame will have to decided and monitored through the different Income Indices as suggested above. In the absence of this, it will be difficult to enhance farmers' income. Mere increase in production and productivity is no guarantee that farmers' income will increase as has happened during the last five years. Government is also seized of this development and has expressed its resolve to double the farmers' income.

It is in this context that targeting increase in farmers' income or doubling it in a given time frame assumes importance. For instance, the per capita average agriculture-GDP was Rs.1503 in Bihar in 2001-02. If it is targeted to double in 2009-10, then Income Indices as mentioned above will have to be compiled and also necessary steps at commodity and non-commodity level will have to be in position so that there is a consistent increase in farmers' income to double it by 2009-10. When the Green Revolution strategy was put into operation target of production of 100 million tonnes food grains was fixed and input package was activated to achieve the target. The extension service was strengthened through TNV (Training and Visit) system for monitoring the supply of inputs and advise to farmers to increase production. On the same pattern, for doubling farmers' income from the present level, appropriate package of income generation will have to designed. Once the income target is quantified it will have to be operationalised by extension services to advise farmers about the supply position of the commodity, likely price he is to receive and other supporting channels available to him. to market his product at best prices. Such a system can be combination of government-private combination such as NGO-farmers' partnership and leading role of farmers' cooperatives. The marginal and small farms where irrigation is not available are mostly of sub-optimal size. They will have to be brought to optimal level by a combination of measures such as contract farming, partnership farming, better marketing support and prices and off-farm and non-farm para-agricultural activities. The extension services associated with income targeting are crucial if sustained increase in farmers' income is to be achieved.

Income Targeting and Monitoring (ITM) is crucial to bring about income revolution for the farmers. When European Union countries faced with problem of falling income of the farmers due to surpluses of agri-produce, they set up a monitoring system and provided special budgetary support. Budget expenditure per commodity was fixed and was made available to each Commodity Market Organization (CMO). Since the number of farmers in EU is small they could afford to give direct payments to farmers. The market price support is still very large for sugar dairy and milk. There are substantial transfers from consumers to farmers which do not appear in budget. The change in budget expenditure reflects a shift from a support funded by consumers to a support funded by tax payers. The price support to farmers and expenses for procurement of surplus produce was funded out of increase in agri-produce and through taxes on consumers. The Commodity Market Organizations guided farmers to have supply control on production vis-à-vis demand and increased sales in domestic and foreign markets. The support to farmers is part of the process of investment to maintain the rural landscape and improving rural infrastructure that generates employment and adds to farmers' income.

Targeting farmers' income and monitoring it will need an organizational set up and investment in rural areas. As mentioned earlier, the investment in agriculture sector is now only 1.5 per cent of GDP and public investment in infrastructure in the sector has not shown any perceptible increase. While direct support to farmers to ensure MSP payment is to be maintained, more will have to be done to set up Commodity Organizations to bring together farmers to organize supply-demand management, promoting demand for their produce in domestic and overseas markets. Such organizations can be funded by farmers themselves by contributing a small fraction of the price of their produce as has been by such organizations in USA and EU. It is not resources alone but great organizational efforts which are needed to improve farmers' income and enrich rural areas.

Some of the huge resources locked up in foreign exchange reserves can be activated to set up fund for targeting and monitoring farmers' income on a sustained basis. Lot of work will have to be done at the State level and by the farmers themselves. A separate Income Fund for Farmers will need financial resources exclusively dedicated for this purpose. A lump sum provision of funds with the provision to re coupe it as the expenses are incurred, is urgently required if the farmers' income is not to deteriorate further. The scheme of such a fund to be financed out of some part of idle foreign exchange reserves is presented in the next Chapter.

Chapter 7

Infrastructure Investment Fund for Farmers (IIFF) Using Foreign Exchange Reserves for Kisans

The investment in agricultural sector has stagnated at 1.3 per cent of GDP during the last three five year plans. Considering the contribution of agriculture to GDP and its employment generation potential, the investment is considered adequate to be at least 6.5 per cent of GDP. Irrigation is the single most important investment that triggers the agrarian prosperity. Out of total net area sown of 140.04 million hectare almost 52 per cent is un-irrigated and 27 per cent is partially irrigated. Only 21 per cent is irrigated. These macro level parameters are more or less true for marginal and small farmers-29 per cent irrigated, 22.2 per cent partially irrigated and 50.2 per cent un-irrigated. As per the Agriculture Census 1995-96, of the 115.58 million operational holdings, 92.8 million are marginal and small holdings and 42.29 million marginal and small holdings have no access to irrigation at all.

In addition, 77 million hectare land is un-utilized and there are vast tracts of land which are known as waste lands which can be developed for cultivation and generation of income and employment. Besides, the large parts of land have degraded and need rehabilitation to its original productivity. Hence there is urgent need to increase investment in agriculture infrastructure.

Irrigation is most critical to income and employment generation in farm sector. Farmers' prosperity crucially depends, inter alia, on availability of irrigation. State-wise percentage coverage of irrigated area under principal crops during 1999-2000 for which the latest data is available shows that for Punjab it is 95.65 per cent, Haryana 85 per cent with lowest for Assam at 5.5 per cent.There is further need to rehabilitate and modernize irrigation tanks and provide funds for minor irrigation projects which need small investment and are labour intensive, quick maturing and are farmer friendly investment for Capital Formation in agriculture.

As mentioned earlier, the Agri-GFCF as percentage of GDP decreased from 1.92 per cent in 1990-91 to 1.31 in 2003-04. The share of private sector GFCF in total GFCF increased from 70.4 per cent to 74.4 per cent during this period but public sector share fell from 29.6 per cent to 25.6 per cent. It may be pointed out that private sector GFCF is limited to plantation sector and does not contribute to rest of the agriculture sector. With the fall in public sector GFCF, the capacity of the agriculture sector is bound to dwindle. This shows that less attention was paid to agriculture sector during the last decade and half.

Recent review Meeting of the Planning Commission held under the Chairmanship of Prime Minister emphasized the need to boost investment in farm sector. In order to give push to agriculture sector the government under its "Bharat Nirman" Scheme has envisaged to bring 10 million hectares under assured irrigation. According to Finance Ministry estimates this will cost Rs.67,000 crores at the rate of Rs.75,000 per hectare for major and medium irrigation projects and Rs.50,000 per hectare for minor irrigation schemes. This will need financial resources of high order which may have to come from non-budgetary sources.

If GFCF is to increase it will need investment resources of long maturity and at low interest rates. But such an arrangement does not exist. If the public sector investment in agri-infrastructure is to increase to 6.5 per cent of GDP, investment fund atleast of the order of Rs.25,000 cro. would be needed in the next three years.

Production Credit to Agriculture Sector

Besides the lagging physical infrastructure in agriculture sector, credit need of the farmers are also not met adequately. Recently two

Committees set up by RBI studied the credit flow to agriculture sector. Prof. Vyas Committee submitted its Report in June 2004. The ground level study pointed out that share of credit going to small farmers is declining. It is only one-fourth of the total credit disbursed. There is need to integrate investment credit and production credit and raising the scale of finance. The linkage between production and marketing and post harvest activities and value addition through agro-processing needs to be strengthened. Committee also emphasized reclamation of wasteland (24.5 million hectare) and fallow land (16 mh) to be brought under cultivation.

The inadequate credit flow has mainly occurred due to erosion of capital base of cooperative credit institutions which has been recently studied by Prof. Vaidyanathan Committee which submitted its report in December 2004. While the network of these banks is wide spread, its business has not remained very effective. There are 1.12 lakh Primary Agriculture Credit Societies (PACs) *i.e.* almost one PAC for every six villages. Total membership of PACs is 12 cror. 36 per cent of the members are SC, ST and small farmers. 62 per cent of PACs are viable, 30 per cent potentially viable and 8 per cent are dormant, defunct or under liquidation. The share of cooperative credit societies decreased from 62 per cent in 1992-93 to 34 per cent in 2002-03 and share of the commercial banks increased from 33 per cent to 57 per cent over the same period. The financial margin of many cooperative credit societies is almost zero and net worth has been eroded. Total accumulated losses of PACs are Rs. 4,595 crores, District Cooperative Credit Societies Rs. 4,401 crores and State Cooperative Banks Rs. 280 crores.

The farmer has still to run to money lender to meet his credit requirement. The 59th Round of National Sample Survey conducted all over India from January to December 2003 has reported that of every Rs. 1000 of outstanding loans of farmers, Rs. 577 was borrowed from banks, cooperative societies and government and the remaining amount from others including money lenders. In the light of these findings it is imperative that credit flow from cooperative societies who have the widest network to reach the farmers must increase urgently.

To revive the Cooperative credit institutions and enable them to help farmers, Committee estimated financial package of Rs.14,839 cro.; Rs.10.839 crores plus Rs. 4000 crores for contingency. The Committee has recommended that 53 per cent of this amount is to be given as grant by Government of India to State governments, 31 per cent as soft loan by GOI to States and 16 per cent as soft loan by GOI to Cooperative Credit Societies. Thus Rs.15,000 cro. are required to revitalize the cooperative credit institutions.

Thus, the total investment fund required for the agriculture sector would be around Rs. 40,000 cro. (Rs. 25,000 cro. GFCF and Rs. 15,000 cro. for capital base of credit societies) at least for the next three to five years.

Inadequate Agri-infrastructure Fund: Current Scenario

The government paid attention to investment in agriculture off late. It set up Rural Infrastructure Development Fund (RIDF) in NABARD in 1995-96 which gives loans to the State governments and State owned cooperatives to complete ongoing projects in irrigation, electricity supply, marketing of agricultural products and tribal welfare. Till 2003-04 nine tranchies of RIDF have been completed. The total corpus of RIDF (1 to 10 trenchies) is Rs.42,000 cro. Cumulative sanctions are of the order of Rs. 37,718 cro. and disbursements amount to Rs. 22.946 cro. as in December 2004. The RIDF investment falls short of requirement besides shortfall in disbursements of RIDF funds. The infrastructure investment of RIDF is thinly spread with the widening of activities of RIDF which include from drinking water to primary school, anganwadies and health centres. Considering the physical infrastructure requirement of agriculture sector and strengthening the cooperative credit institutions as detailed above, RIDF falls much short of requirement and its spread is thin to strengthening agriculture infrastructure. There are enough irrigation and other agri-infrastructure projects on shelf with State Govts and have good institutional arrangements to implement. Since the State Govts. are saddled with huge debt burden and lack investment funds, they may be slack in farm sector infrastructure investment. If the funds become available at low interest rate and for long maturity period, the States will come forward to increase agri-infrastructure.

Can the funds be raised from any other sources? Is there such a source available?

Investment Fund Available: Share in Idle Foreign Exchange Reserves

India has accumulated foreign exchange reserves (FER) of $140 billion equivalent to about Rs. 6 lakh cro. They have been sterilized. Large part of FER is non-debt creating except NRI deposits of about $30 bn which means there is no fear of flight of foreign exchange. Thus huge financial resources are available but are not being used for fear of increase in inflation with the conversion of dollar into rupees.

Considering the need to utilize the idle FER, Dy. Chairman, Planning Commission, took up the issue with the Ministry of Finance of utilizing FER for increasing investment in industrial infrastructure. Appreciating this novel move, the Finance Minister in his Budget 2005-06 has made provision of funding viable infrastructure projects through Special Purpose Vehicle (SPV) for utilizing FER for required imports in roads, ports, airports and tourism sectors. The SPV will lend fund especially debt of long term maturity directly to the eligible projects to supplement other loans. A provision of Rs.10,000 cro. has been made for 2005-06. When FER can be used for industrial infrastructure investment, then why not for investment in farm sector for prosperity of farmers ?

It is against this background that there is strong case for utilizing FER for investment in irrigation, land development and imports needed to strengthen the investment in marketing of agri-produce nationally and internationally-at concessional interest rate with a maturity period (20-25 years) through SPV.

Foreign Exchange Reserves Scenario: Case for utilization for Agri-Investment Fund

According to the latest Report of the Reserve Bank of India on Foreign Exchange Reserves (September 2005 published in Jan'06), total FER were $143.1 billion (now about $154.1 billion in April 2006). Of this, Foreign Currency Asset (FCA) are 95 per cent. FCA is a multi-currency portfolio in US$, Pound Sterling, Euro, Japanese Yen etc. In 2004-05, Foreign Direct Investment (FDI) amount was $5.5 billion, NRI Deposits $32.8 billion, Cumulative Foreign Institutional Investment $35.9 billion by end March 2005 and $40.3 billion by end September 2005.

India is in a very comfortable position of FER. It gives a cover for 14.3 months imports by end 2005 and 11.2 months end September 2005, while the normal requirement is 5/6 months imports. The other parameters on the external front are comfortable and are within safe limits. India's concessional debt is 35 per cent and short term debt to total debt is 5.3 per cent in March 2005 amd 5.8 per cent end September 2005, as per the latest data available. External debt to GDP is now only 17.8 per cent. The emphasis is on non-debt creating capital flows. With the huge accumulation of FER government has made pre-payment of high interest cost debt of $7.68 billion during 2002-03 to 2004-05. IMF has designated India as a creditor under Financial Transaction Plan (FTP) in February 2003. India has now provided financial support to Burundi during March-May 2003 and a contribution of SDR 5 million and to Brazil in June 2003 with SDR 350 million. In December 2003, SDR 43 million was made available to Indonesia under FTP. The total amount under FTP was SDR 398 million by end September 2004.

According to the latest Report (January 2006) of the RBI on Foreign Exchange Reserves "the significant increase in forex reserves enabled prepayment of certain high-cost foreign currency loans of the Government of India from the Asian Development Bank (ADB) and the World Bank (IBRD) amounting to US$ 3.03 billion during February 2003. During 2003-04, prepayment of certain high cost loans to IBRD and ADB amounting to US$ 2.6 billion was carried out by the Government. Additionally, prepayment of bilateral loans amounting to US$ 1.1 million was also made. Thus, the total quantum of prepayments was of the order of US$ 3.7 billion during 2003-04. During 2004-05, prepayment of bilateral loan to the tune of US$ 30.3 million was made. During April-September 2005, no prepayment of high-cost multilateral/bilateral loan was carried out."

The present management of external front is very prudent. The current exchange rate policy focuses on managing volatility with no fixed rate target. Allowing the underlying demand and supply conditions to determine the exchange rate movements in an orderly way has stood the test of time. The Indian rupee has appreciated against US dollar and the rate has touched the highest at $= Rs.43.43. Inspite of this comfortable position, FER have remained unutilized.

The FER to a large extent is sterilized by RBI as its conversion to Indian rupees will increase the money supply leading to high inflation in the economy. The investment pattern and earnings from FER shows that the return on FCA and gold, after accounting for depreciation, decreased to 2.1 per cent in 2003-04 from 3.1 per cent during 2002-03 mainly because of lower money market interest in major countries and fall in prices of securities due to rise in longer term yields. The opportunity cost of using FER is only 3.1 per cent.

The recent move by the Dy. Chairman, Planning Commission, to sponsor the utilization of FER for industrial infrastructure investment on long maturity with lower interest under Special Purpose Vehicle (SPV) is recognition of the fact that there is no imminent fear of foreign exchange crisis and apprehension of inflation should not be deterrent to use FER on moderate scale. In addition, opportunity cost of FER is 3.1 per cent only.

Though in principle it is envisaged that SPV of Rs. 10,000 cro. will be used for imports and hence there will not be any inflationary impact may not come out to be true. While the amount for civil aviation is spent on purchase of air crafts, its multiplier effect will increase spending in Indian rupees on expansion of civil aviation activities. This will add to money supply. Construction of roads will hardly need imports as most of the inputs are domestic and expenditure on roads will add to money supply. Taking a modest multiplier factor of three, the use of foreign exchange reserves of Rs.10,000 cro. of SPV may lead to increase in expenditure of Rs.30,000 cro. which can have some inflationary impact.

Infrastructure Investment Fund for Farmers (IIFF)

In the light of the above facts and model set for utilization of FER for industrial infrastructure through SPV, there is every justification to create Infrastructure Investment Fund for Farmers to increase flow of fund to boost capital formation and for rehabilitating cooperative credit institutions at grass root level as detailed above. Initially, corpus fund of Rs. 50,000 cro. (about $10 billion) may be created out of FER for a period five years and after getting an experience of IIFF, it can be converted in a permanent institutional arrangement for financing infrastructure investment in agriculture by opening a line of credit from FER on a regular basis. The financing pattern of IIFF is to be of long maturity period (20 to 25 years) and low interest rates (around 2 to 4 per cent) to the State government and other implementing agencies. The initial institutional arrangement may be done on the pattern of SPV set up for industrial infrastructure created in the Budget 2005-06. In the beginning the utilization will be moderate at about a billion dollars as it will take time to be ready with viable project proposals. Over time the utilization will pick up. The Fund is to be made available to the State governments on the pattern of IDA of the World Bank with the same drill of project preparation and implementation.

In fact, much needed capital by the cooperative credit institutions financed by IIFF will put life in to rural credit system. The IIFF can be urgently used for rehabilitating PACs, DCCS and SCCS by providing grants and soft loans as recommended by Vaidyanathan Committee. This will provide much needed funds by small farmers for production and marketing. Early completion of irrigation projects, development of lands and wastelands and other activities will generate employment and income in agriculture sector. As long as increase in money supply is matched by increase in agriculture produce, the rate of inflation will not increase.

Cooling Inflation

One of the objections that may be raised against IIFF being created out of FER is that the money in circulation will increase leading to inflationary pressures. In this connection it should be understood that inflation is a macro phenomena. Spending on agriculture infrastructure alone need not be the cause of inflation. In the recent past inflation touched 8 per cent level due to steep increase in petroleum prices. The RBI is more concerned that money in circulation should not be cause of inflation and this is the right monetary policy also. But there are various other factors that lead to non-RBI inflation due to supply demand position in the market.

In regard to IIFF, when the investment funds will be spent mainly in rural areas, it will provide employment to unemployed and under employed rural labour who will spend large amount on food and daily necessities. There is huge supply of food grains available that will negate the influence of increased money supply and cool down the inflation substantially. There is abundance of inputs for creating infrastructure such as steel, cement etc. that will also taper of inflationary effect of such a spending. Timely availability of credit will help in increasing agriculture production and thereby arresting the price rise.

The needed imports for agriculture sector for value added exports will add to foreign exchange earnings recouping part of FER used for IIFF. The agro-based activities will get boost which will increase supplies of poultry, milk, fruits and vegetables and processed foods. The Director General of Foreign Trade (DGFT) issued a public notice on April 27th 2005 listing entry of these items for duty free license at 5 per cent of export value. The Scheme-Videsh Krishi Upaj Yojana–covers last year's exports and current year's exports. The KNUY license will trade at small discount on the duty credit entitlement.

In addition, modern marketing systems can be installed overseas using these funds for disposal of surplus agriculture produce. It may be pointed that a new development on product-based trade pacts is emerging. The proposal on product-specific trade liberalization has been mooted jointly by the US and Canada. Government is examining this proposal. The product trade pacts for surplus wheat, rice, sugar, cotton and fruits and vegetable using IIFF can be pushed that will increase agriculture production mitigating the inflationary pressure.

It may be pointed that as per the press reports, about $3 to 4 billion of NRI's Savings Bank Account are converted into Indian rupees for purchase of real estates and other investment. So, the money in circulation is increasing almost by Rs.9000 to Rs.10,000 cro. Insipte of this, the inflation is under control. These investments are in the nature of financial transactions and hardly add to production.

Provision of assured irrigation on 10 million hectares envisaged in "Bharat Nirman" Scheme by 2009 financed from IIFF will boost agriculture production which will work as shield against inflation and serve as safety net. After all the funds under IIFF will not be spent in one go. IIFF will be spent in small to medium doses of investment.

India is not the first country to use its FER for infrastructure investment. The Chinese government used FER of $45 billion to fund a new institution, the Central Huijin Investment Company, like our SPV, which in turn funded the Bank of China and China Construction Bank for infrastructure development. In December 2003, the Bank of China and China Construction Bank received $22 billion each to clean up their balance sheets and prepare them for listing on stock exchange. Recently in April 2005 Chinese government authorized a $15 billion bailout package to financially weak lender–Industrial and Commercial Bank of China-(ICBs).

Government has initiated process for operating the SPV for industrial infrastructure investment. A proposal to this effect is to be approved by the Cabinet and thereafter SPV would get registered as a company. As per the information available, Rs.10,000 cro. SPV paper to finance infrastructure development are expected to be priced at about 100 basis points, above government paper. At current rates, 10 year debt paper to be issued by the SPV would therefore carry a coupon rate of 8.4 per cent while a 15 year paper is likely to be priced at less than 7.4 per cent; so the SPV paper does not become competitor of government securities. Despite this, SPV paper would still be attractive investment avenues for the capital market. The higher interest rate for SPV is necessary as it could otherwise create difficulties for the government's borrowing programme. SPV will carry quasi government guarantee. This makes SPV almost at par with the central government paper. The rates would be much lower than the ones which infrastructure projects have to normally factor in. Most infrastructure projects carry higher interest rates which are either equal to Prime Lending Rate (PLR) or more depending on the profile of the borrowers. The strategy of using FER for IIFF would provide returns from infrastructure development in agriculture sector. The return would definitely be significantly higher than the returns (2.1 per cent) from US or Euro deposits where our reserves are currently parked.

Financing Income Targeting and Monitoring

The IIFF is an institutional arrangement that will have to be operated by the Union Ministry of Agriculture in consultations with the State governments. A Governing Council of IIFF can mainly concentrate on Income Targeting and Monitoring Schemes. They can specifically deal with the areas having a bearing on income management for the farmers and providing them collective assets that will increase their income and improve marketability of their produce.

Increasing Agri-GDP

As pointed earlier the per capita agri-GDP in rural sector depends upon the size of the total agri-GDP that will overtake the rate of growth of rural population. A phased program of investment to boost agri-GDP in lowest ranked States (per capita agri-GDP) can be financed from IIFF at very low rate of interest (2 to 4 per cent) for a maturity period of 20 to 25 years. Such programs can be funded on project basis for States like Bihar and Orissa on priority to benefit the farmers. The Central and State agencies engaged in the procurement have to increase net work to protect the farmers from falling prices. Some financial assistance at concessional interest and long maturity period can be lent to such agencies for effective protection to farmers.

Commodity Organizations

Commodity Organizations of farmers at the Apex and State level are going to play a pivotal role in supply management and marketing of agriculture produce in the future. Realizing this importance these organizations can be provided start up grants from IIFF and concessional loan finance. These institutional developments will need soft lending in the initial phases. Later on farmers themselves will raise their resources as has been done by such organizations in developed countries. One time marketing grants to Commodity Boards can be given equivalent to the amount of their own collection of funds.

Compensatory Finance for Marketing Reforms

The State governments are regulating the agri-produce markets under APMA. The reforming of APMA on the pattern of the Model APMA of the Central government may lead to some revenue loss to the State governments. The compensatory finance in the form of soft loans to States governments will give sufficient breathing time to them to carry out the reforms quickly benefiting the farmers by reducing cost of marketing. This off-budget soft loan finance will accelerate in developing alternate marketing for the farmers.

Model Agro-Industries at Farm Gates

The radial agro-industrialization at the farm gates enunciated in Chapter III can be started on a pilot basis involving corporate sector and NGOs on a BOT basis by financing from IIFF on very concessional terms besides the tax and other concessions. The State governments and farmers' Commodity Organizations can be made partners in this experiment of agro-industrialization at the farm gates. Farmers will see for themselves the benefits of farm gate activity which has multiplier effect of providing local employment and developing the skills.

Emergency Direct Payment to Farmers

Farmers face fall in income due to draught or flood or any other calamities. Central and State governments provide relief by way of waiving interest payment, electricity bills etc. But that hardly gives direct income to the farmer who is in distress. In such cases, farmers can be given income equivalent to 2/3rd of last year's value of his produce as a soft loan at 1 or 2 per cent interest for a maturity period of five years. This will protect from the distress and arrange for his livelihood more respectfully than receiving above mentioned relief. Such direct payments can be ear marked for each year as contingency direct payments to farmers.

The activating of idle foreign exchange reserves of the order of \$10 to \$15 billion (about Rs. 65,000 to Rs.70,000 cro.) as corpus fund for setting up IIFF would be financially viable proposition in terms of return on such funds parked abroad. India was competing to get more concessional funds from International Development Association (IDA), soft lending arm of the World Bank. Now government has comfortable foreign exchange reserves and small part of it *i.e.* about 10 per cent, can be used for benefiting the farmers who are feeding India's teeming million. Bold decision is required to allay the fear of inflation and eroding foreign exchange reserves.

Chapter 8

Welcome to WTO: Farmers Ready to Meet the Challenge

The setting up of World Trade Organization (WTO) in 1995 replacing the General Agreement Tariffs and Trade (GATT) has expanded the coverage of trade to services and is introducing further trade liberalization in goods and factors of production. It is not the physical movement of goods alone but the services which have not now remained location specific. In spite of industrialization all over the world, agriculture is still the back bone not only of developing countries but of developed countries. The production and trade in agricultural commodities in developed countries is far more protected than in developing countries. This has become the bone of contention between the developed and the developing countries. The farmers with slender land base find it difficult to compete with the subsidized trade of the developed countries in agricultural commodities.

Indian farmers in present state of affairs are on a sound footing to compete with the developed countries' subsidized trade and more so to find access to their domestic markets. The institutional arrangements, proper pricing, cost effective marketing and financial reforms and mechanism to index and monitor farmers' income enunciated in the previous Chapters will make farmers much stronger economically to welcome the WTO initiated trade reforms. As revealed in the 59th Round of the NSSO only 8 per cent of the farmers are aware about the existence of the WTO. But with concerted efforts to bring farmers into domestic and international marketing and trading system, they can face the challenge boldly. India's agriculture and farmers are not protected compared to their counterparts in developed countries and are working in free trade environment. While developed countries are under obligation to dismantle the subsidies that protect their production and exports, India has already liberalized its trade in agriculture production and exports. Almost all the trade and non-trade barriers have been removed. India's agriculture subsidies are peanut compared to EU, USA and Japan. This can be seen from the Table 14.

Table 14: Agricultural Subsidies in India and Developed Countries ($ billion)

Country	*1999-2000*	*2001-02*
India	6.87	8.05
EU	115.33	93.08
USA	55.43	49.00
Japan	53.80	47.24

Source: Agricultural Statistics At A Glance 2004. Ministry of Agri. & cooperation.

Table 14 shows the large amount of subsidies paid to agricultural sector in EU, USA and Japan compared to India. Not only this, farmers in these countries receive large amount of Producer Support (PS) which indicates the annual value of gross transfers from consumers and tax payers to agricultural producers, measured at the farm gate level, arising from policy measures that support agriculture, regardless of their nature, objectives or impact on farm production or income. It is expressed as percentage of gross farm receipts that shows the amount of support to farmers, irrespective of the sectoral structure of a given country. The PS *i.e.* direct receipts of the farmers in EU is 35 per cent of total subsidies, USA 21 per cent and Japan 59 per cent.

As reported in various reports and studies and brought out in Time Magazine (November 28, 2005), Caribean sugar farmers can not compete with European farms that benefit from generous crop subsidies. EU was the largest importer of Sugar 30 years back. It is now the largest exporter of sugar. Sugar made from beet is produced in such in-hospitable areas like Finland. This is hurting the poorest countries who are much suited to produce sugar such as Haiti, Mozambique and Thailand. Rich countries spend more than $300 billion a year on agriculture as "producer support". World Bank Chief Economist estimates that a European cow receives $2.50 per day by subsidies while 75 per cent of Africans live on less than $2 a day. With huge subsidies paid to farmers air conditioned tractors are common in farms of EU and USA. In a world of Ricardian economics which the WTO is endeavoring to create, West African farmers would be thriving. They are capable of producing high quality cotton more cheaply compared to USA which is subsidizing high cost cotton cultivation. Cultivation of subsidized cotton started in USA and the sales were mere 17 per cent of world exports in 1998 which have now increased to 41 per cent in 2003. Due to this, the world prices of cotton have dropped by more than half. Developed countries make a pledge of higher aid to developing countries. The cotton farmers of the developing countries have lost $ 23 billion during the past four years to western subsidies. The loss is almost equal to US aid donations. Burkina Faso received $ 10 million in US aid in 2002 but lost an estimated $14 million in cotton exports because of US cotton subsidies.

It is in this trade environment that the Indian farmer is to compete in a WTO regime. Compared to this Indian farmer hardly gets any direct receipts out of the agricultural subsidies. The agri-subsidy in India is mainly for fertilizer, electricity and irrigation. Other subsidies given to marginal farmers and farmers' cooperatives in the form of seeds, development of seeds, pulses etc. amounted to Rs. 978 cro. (2.6 per cent) out of total subsidy of Rs. 36,224 cro. in 2001-02. Therefore, against this background of subsidization of farmers in developed countries India is hardly a subsidized country. Hence, there is need to make Indian farmer economically strong by increasing his income through domestic policies of better pricing for his produce, cost effective marketing, organizing him in Commodity Boards and finding market for his surplus production. Before this is brought into the focus of WTO framework it will be useful to take bird's eye view of Agreement on Agriculture of WTO that has yet not been ratified by the developed countries. India's position against this backdrop and the way the Indian farmers can benefit from these developments are presented below.

WTO Regime

The rules of the game of international trade followed individually and collectively have been bone of contention amongst the trading nations. Three factors are at the root cause of such a state of affairs. In the first place, the levels of economic development amongst nations differ widely, secondly cost of production differs due to asymmetrical factor endowment amongst nations and thirdly nations restrict or encourage trade in goods and services and manipulate domestic production structure, even at the cost of becoming uneconomic, to mop up gains to themselves. Before World War II, there was no collective body of nations which could frame mutually agreed rules of international trade that will benefit all nations. After WW II, an international trade organization namely General Agreements on Tariffs and Trade (GATT) was set up which laid down the rules of foreign trade in goods. Trade in services was outside the purview of GATT.

Another important development in Europe in late 50's to expand the markets was free trade within Europe but protection from outside with high tariffs and quota. The economic basis for this model of free trade and protection was small book of Swedish Prof. and Economist J E Meade titled Customs Union which laid the foundation of European Common Market (ECM), now European Union (EU) with all its concomitant policies of protected agriculture trade.

This arrangement worked well till 1980s. But with the development of less developed countries the competition increased and the trade barriers of developed countries became oppressive to them. In the intervening period since GATT did not lay down the rules of trade in services, now mainly termed as Intellectual Property Rights (IPRs), the developing countries started taking advantage and improved their technical comparative cost advantage. Trade regime became more protective at the one end and informally free on the other end resulting in losses to the trading partners. There arose need to recast GATT to attend to the complicated trade regimes. The developed and developing countries held a series of meetings to evolve a new trade order for the benefit of all. Thus World Trade Organization (WTO) came into existence on 1st January 1995.

WTO Agreement on Agriculture (AoA)

Without getting in to entire gamut of various WTO Agreements, the agreement engaging serious attention of developed and developing countries in the recent past is AoA. The discussions and the Meetings held for AoA have been highly controversial and timetable laid down for finalizing the AoA has not been followed. Before the AoA proper is considered relating to India's trade and its perspective reflected in Doha, Cancun and Hong Kong Meetings of WTO, it will be in order to understand why agriculture is at stake and dear to industrialized developed countries where share of agriculture GDP out of total GDP is around 5 to 10 per cent. Why do they provide high financial support to agriculture sector in general and agriculture export in particular ?

In this connection, it is interesting to note that of the top 15 agriculture goods exporters, value of exports of EU Members is $215 billion out of total value of $445 bn (39 per cent) and USA $70 bn (12.8). Agriculture products share in exports in 2001 in North America is 58.3 per cent and Western Europe 56 per cent. In import of agriculture products share of North America is 32.7 per cent and Western Europe 56.6 per cent. This indicates that industrialized developed countries' trade in agriculture is of high magnitude and their economies are intimately linked to agriculture sector though share of agriculture GDP in total GDP may be low at around 10 per cent and population in agriculture sector is just around 2 to 4 per cent.

The entire agriculture edifice in developed countries like EU, USA and Japan and others is supported by direct financial assistance to farmers. This is circular flow of income from non-farm sector to farm sector and that too adding directly to income of the farmers and infrastructure and landscaping of rural hinterland. It is also to be noted that the developed countries close down the factory if it is comparatively disadvantageous to produce the good in question and even resort to out sourcing. But they are not ready to get comparatively cheap food and agriculture goods from developing countries by relaxing and dismantling barriers to agriculture trade for the reason that direct support to farmers of transferring income from non-farm sector and maintaining agriculture infrastructure and beautiful landscapes will be disturbed. The reason to make a detour to this scenario in developed countries is to understand why there is go slow on AoA by developed countries vis-à-vis developing countries who are demanding early implementation of AoA to eliminate trade distorting effects on their economies.

AoA: Where are We ?

The genesis of subsidizing agricultural primary products goes back to 1947 when GATT allowed countries to use export subsidies on agricultural primary products but export subsidies on industrial products were prohibited. This resulted in proliferation of impediments to world agriculture trade. Developed countries used export subsidies to dump their surpluses on the world market depressing world market prices. Their high domestic support to agriculture encouraged over-production leading to low levels of international prices. America's 25,000 cotton farmers received $3 billion (about Rs.13,500 crores *i.e.* Rs.5.4 million per farmer) and can therefore out produce and undersell 11 million people of west Africa who depend on cotton for their main source of income.

Total domestic support to farm sector in OECD countries which was $308 billion in 1986 has gone upto $361 billion which is six times the total value of the current annual agriculture GDP and over three times India's current foreign exchange reserves of $140 billion. At the time of setting up of WTO in 1995, the average tariffs in OECD were 214 per cent for wheat, 197 per cent barley, 154 per cent maize. In EU countries, tariff quota for bananas is 180 per cent Japan 460 to 600 per cent for dried beans and lentils, USA groundnut in shells 164 per cent. Recently, Japan has levied a tariff of about 1000 per cent on rice. This situation has not changed much. The production and export of many agriculture commodities by developed countries is like producing "Grapes" in glass houses when the natural conditions may not support such a production. Developed countries do not want to dismantle their "glass houses" of farmers even when farm production is uneconomic.

When developed countries were building such domestic supports and erecting tariff walls, the developing countries in 1950s were hardly visible on the map of food grains production and agriculture products. They were net importers. It was only around mid 1980s when Green Revolution made India and developing countries competitive on farm sector front when India's then Finance Minister in 1986 raised the issue that "Agriculture should be brought within the purview of GATT due to extensive subsidization by the developed countries which led to distortion in prices of agriculture commodities". But scenario continues to be as detailed above. It is this situation that is to be corrected in AoA. The journey of AoA from

Uruguay to Doha and further to Cancun as in August 2003 and in Hong Kong in December 2005 is detailed in Annex VI.

The results of WTO Hong Kong are very modest as no significant agreements could be reached. The date of meeting the target of reducing subsidies and restrictions of tariffs of the developed countries has now been postponed to 2013. The debt relief to African countries is hardly round the corner. Most of the debt relief will go to Nigeria and Iraq who have not even serviced their debts. Even if the debt is cancelled poorer nations may have to agree to remove trade barriers, which means competing with subsidized western products, leaving the farmers at the mercy of world market. Make Poverty History (MPH), an organization of the G8 to help the African countries seeks end to subsidies that damage the livelihood of the poorest. At the WTO Hong Kong Conference it became clear that the main trading nations are years away from agreeing a deal to end subsidies and lower tariffs. Deadlock continues over $300 billion subsidies of EU, USA and Japan. Export subsidies are less than 5 per cent of the total subsidies which encourages EU and USA farmers to flood the world market with cheap goods. Hence not much relief from developed countries can be expected is the message of the WTO.

Given the stalemate and postponement of implementation of AoA by developed countries till 2013, India will have to develop its own strategy by remodeling agricultural sector that will increase agri-GDP, increase domestic and foreign demand for its agri-products and thereby increasing farmers' income in given time frame to make them competitive in the world market. A complete turn round will be needed to shift emphasis from production to income of the farmers without which market expansion in the domestic economy will not take place. Economically weak farmers can hardly compete in the world market howsoever agriculture production may increase. Large chunk of farmers and rural population can not be left behind if India is to compete in the world market. Before a new strategy is spelled out it will be useful to look into India's position in the WTO regime.

India's Position

India stands out as the least protected and is within the frame work of WTO parameters of AoA. Indian subsidy is well below the ceiling prescribed in Uruguay Round. India does not provide any product specific support other than market price support. Except for tobacco and sugarcane, international prices of all products were higher than the domestic prices, hence negative. Non-product specific subsidy of Rs.4585 crores is well within minimus level. India has no reduction commitment. There are no direct subsidies for agricultural commodities. Only subsidy is exemption of export profits from income tax and subsidies on cost of freight on export shipment of certain products like fruits, vegetables and floriculture products.

AoA does not require India to reduce the existing subsidies for research, pest and disease control, marketing and promotion of services and infrastructure support services. PDS is not a subsidy for farmers or producer. Consumer subsidies are exempt from WTO. India's food security remains unaffected. Three additional exemptions available to developing countries namely investment subsidies, agriculture input subsidy and domestic support to producers to encourage diversification from growing narcotics are available to India also. India also gets benefit of Article C.2 of WTO which allows additional support for rural development for low income and resource poor producers and for crops grown as substitutes for narcotics.

Thus, India is on a strong wicket in so far as its commitment to AoA is concerned. But India is not in a position to realize perceived benefits of implementation of AoA by the developed countries that will provide market access to India's agriculture exports which have a competitive edge. Insipte of India's efforts for special and differential treatment in Doha, Cancun and Hong Kong Conferences nothing much has materialized.

Remodeling Agrarian Strategy

The production oriented Green Revolution strategy seems to have lost its thrust to make agriculture a resilient force to face international trade and make farmers economically well off. In a market oriented world economy under WTO regime and globalization forces in particular, agriculture strategy needs to be remodeled to shift emphasis from production to farmers' income and comprehensive rural development. India is to compete with big trading blocks of EU and USA in the future and especially trade in agriculture. The biggest trade block is EU. The exports of EU were $ 2747 billion in 2004 and imports were $ 2735 billion. India' exports to EU were $ 20 billion and imports from EU were $20.2 billion. Such is the vast trading difference between India and group of countries in EU.

The orientation of investment will have to change so that in spite of structural differences India should be able to compete with EU and USA. The package of inputs and extension services enabled marginal and small farmers to achieve self sufficiency in food grains and increase food grains exports considerably. But to face future challenges remodeling of agrarian strategy is required. It will be helpful to see what are the structural differences between India, EU and USA under which India's new agrarian strategy is to take shape.

Table 15: Structure of the Economies of India, EU and USA, 2003

Sl.No.	Item	India	EU (25 countries)	USA
1.	Area (million hectare)	141.1	183.7	477.2
2.	Population (million)	1028.7	453.7	290.8
3.	No. of holdings (million)	115.5	5.35	2.2
4.	Av. Farm Size (hectare)	1.41	10-57	224.0
5.	Share of Agri in GDP (%)	20.0	1.6	2.0
6.	Employment in Agri (million)	234.1*	10.1	2.3
7.	Share of Agri-imports in total Imports (%)	4.5	6.4	4.2
8.	Share of Agri-exports in total Exports (%)	12.4	6.5	9.3

* Cultivators and Agri-labourers. Total rural population 742.6 million.

Source: Basic Data: Key General Statistics: European Commission Agriculture Statistics At A Glance: Ministry of Agriculture.

Table 15 shows the structural difference between India, EU and USA mainly in regard to huge population depending on agriculture as a source of livelihood and small size of holdings. There are only 10 million and 2 million persons employed in agriculture in EU and USA respectively compared to 234 million in India. India's total rural population of 762 million is equal to total population of EU and USA put together. Such is the dimension of economic parameters in which India has to compete in WTO regime and the subsidized agriculture sector of these two big traders in the world. Not much trade relief in agriculture sector is expected till 2013 when the developed countries have to make their economies de-subsidize. Hence India will have to develop its own strategy to increase trade in agricultural commodities and increase farmers' Income. It is a stupendous task and needs remodeling of agrarian changes making Indian agriculture more marketable and income generating. There are two aspects to this strategy which was described earlier as commodity and non-commodity areas that will have to be addressed.

Produce and Convert for Market

The production and trading pattern of developed countries significantly moved away from primary production to processing and quality improvement and under-selling wherever such approach did not help. The raw cotton and sugar are sold with heavy subsidy to maintain farmers' income and employment and other products such as milk, meat etc are processed and then sold in different markets. India tried successfully such a strategy by converting cotton and other textiles to manufacturing readymade garments and apparels selling them in domestic and more aggressively in foreign markets. If such a shift would not have been made there would have been a glut in textiles and prices would have fallen. The decentralized production of readymade garments in private sector provided employment far and wide and by reducing overhead costs, the small units produced readymade garments at competitive costs. In addition, the foreign markets were captured by appropriately producing garments that would meet the tastes of the foreign buyers through institutional and fiscal support. This established India as the major exporter and competitor of readymade garments in the world market. The small firms did this miracle. The strategy of "textiles to readymade garments" captured the world market that displaced Koreans and Japanese. Similarly Indian gold and jewelry artists were organized to produce gold and diamond jewelry that met the tastes and quality required by foreign consumers. It provided employment and income to small artisans and is earning huge foreign exchange. Such a strategy needs to be adopted in agricultural sector.

The agri-commodities in primary form face the problem of glut in market and fall in prices but if such commodities are processed as ready-food or ready-to-eat food for domestic and foreign consumers, it can provide employment, generate exports and add to farmers' income. This will need a lot of initiative from the government in initial stages and building of institutional support to identify tastes of foreign consumers and establishing trade channels besides fiscal incentives for a specified period. This is what is envisaged in Radial Agro-processing at Farm Gate enunciated in Chapter III. Small and medium level food and vegetable processors meeting the quality requirements like that of the readymade garment manufacturers can flood the domestic and foreign markets. Such a change does not attract WTO regime. Readymade or Ready-To-Eat Food is staple diet of most of the foreign consumers and when their tastes and quality standards are met, Indian farmers can make in-road in to world market as has been made by readymade garment manufactures. A big push is required to operationalize the "Produce and Convert for Market" Strategy to accommodate the rural population in rural areas with farmers on the vanguard. Let the developed countries continue their policy of go slow on subsidy to their agriculture sector. That should not deter India in remodeling its agrarian strategy in changed circumstances.

Farming for Foreign Consumers

The consumers in EU, USA and other developed countries are switching to organic products right from food to textile and this is a great potential market. Their import of organic products is increasing. They have started converting their land from chemical agriculture to organic farming and are providing incentives to the farmers. By the time they dismantle their tariffs on import of agriculture products and subsidies to farmers, these countries will have switched over to organic farming and organic products. Much before the WTO was set up, the EU countries started promoting Organic Farming (OF) to reduce costs of inputs, favouring higher employment and produce consumer friendly products for which there is a growing demand. EU imports organic agriculture products from non-member countries and 70 per cent of demand is met from imports. It all started in 1992 by encouraging conversion from chemical agriculture to organic agriculture that may not attract the IPRs and provides protection and income to small farmers. EU's Rural Development Regulation administers this scheme in Member countries. Since 1992, 15 EU countries have converted 33.35 lakh hectares of land to organic farming. Brief particulars of conversion to Organic Farming in EU are given in Annexure VII. The day will not be far away when EU will go for organic farming and will not need food produced that uses chemicals in developing countries in the next decade. By then the EU may reduce trade tariffs as per AoA.

At that stage non-organic produce of developing countries will not have much demand in these countries. India can take advantage of this change in consumption pattern of foreign consumers by contracting for bulk orders of organic agriculture products. India still produces and has the capacity to produce organic agri-produce and can meet the quality standards of foreign consumers. Such a captive demand for the dedicated farming will help increase employment and income of the farmers. Such a selective transformation to organic farming for a long period will make the foreign consumers attached to Indian products. This is a singular opportunity which the Indian farmers should not miss. The government intervention is urgently required for this far sighted strategy. This is an area of government initiatives.

Internalizing IPRs: Organic Farming

Organic farming will reduce dependence of farmers on biotechnology and large MNCs' monopolizing seed industry. Farmers will be able to save and reuse harvested material for the next season and farmers are free to use seeds from a protected variety for sowing without the permission from PBR holders besides saving in input cost.

When Organic Farming in EU countries is freely operating without infringing IPRs and is falling explicitly outside the support system why not India also integrate its Protection of Plant Varieties and Farmers Act 2001 and Biological Rights Act 2001 in organic farming by institutionalizing it as has been done by EU countries since 1992. This will obviate and control the role of monopoly of seed companies. Such an integration will be most suitable for large number of farmers of dry farming and rain fed areas. The details can be worked out and lessons can be learnt from EU. The targets for conversion to organic farming and exports of organic agri-produce for which there is great demand from EU can also be fixed as has been done in EU countries.

In addition to this, the compensation paid for converting to organic farming in EU countries transfers income from non-farm economy to farmers and generating more employment in rural areas.

Such a scheme can be implemented in India which is the dire need in the present circumstances. This should fit into WTO framework also.

Public research can also divert its attention and resources to organic farming without infringing IPRs. Let MNCs do biological research and compete with local scheme of organic farming. The public sector research should aid and assist the inputs required for organic farming and leave most of the biotech research to private activities and collaboration that will benefit the farmers from irrigated areas.

India's Initiatives: Tackling IPRs

Since nothing much can be done on market access immediately relating to domestic support measures and export subsidies of the developed countries except building pressure through G-20, India needs to concentrate on areas which are within its own domain. One such area of importance and having far reaching effects is orienting IPRs in its own favour.

Article 27 of TRIPs requires Member states to allow patents for any invention "whether product or process in all fields of technology". In plant varieties, countries have choice *i.e.* protect these either through patents or devise a sui generis system, suitable for their own requirements. India may not be able to do much on patent protection to life forms, including micro-organisms and micro-biological processes as it has to fall in line with Article 27 of TRIPs.

Protection of Plant Varieties and Farmers' Rights Act 2001 and Biological Diversity Bill 2001 safeguard the small farmers based on sui generis principle though there will always be pressure groups of MNCs who will try to make in-roads. In order to Indianise the benefits of these measures further, it will be helpful if India links it to promoting new approach to farming that will reduce cost, increase income and employment.

TRIPs as applied to agriculture forces developing countries to extend IPRs to plant varieties and seeds. This is demanded by the innovators of developed countries as PBRs with breeders' exemptions and farmers' privilege are not sufficient to recoup their huge investment in R&D to develop these inventions. Insistence of implementation of WTO TRIPS related to agriculture is asking developing countries to finance expenses of R&D whether developing countries want their innovations or not. It is globalization of agriculture at the cost of developing countries.

No Costs No TRIPs

Agriculture is vastly different in India *i.e.* from dry farming to rain fed to irrigation based. Input package applicable to irrigated farming is not applicable to dry farming and rain fed. Sui generis application of TRIPs for these different types of farming can be devised. Since the farmers income base is very weak in later areas, their innovations need not be patented as most of these are presently traded amongst themselves without consideration of any payments. More so, local innovations do not involve any huge expenditure on R&D. What objection there should be if small farmers share their innovations with each other without detriment to developed countries' innovation. If there is virtually no cost to innovator and if the innovator like the small Indian farmer does not want to go in for patent, it should not attract TRIPs.

In fact innovators in EU and other developed countries hold regular TV shows to popularize innovations of localized nature for adoption by others to reduce costs or increase in income. That does not attract TRIPs. Similarly innovation by small farmers and shared with each other need not attract TRIPs. TRIPs should be applicable only when developing countries are pirating the innovations of developed countries. That should not be allowed. But to bring the farmers' local methods of farming using their own seeds and sharing those with others is far fetched application of TRIPs.

Instead of patents for innovations at individual farmers levels, it can be registered as Farmers' Patents Collectively and traded with developed countries by the government. If they wish to use these innovations and pay for it, the amount so received can be put in Farmers' Innovation Fund for rewarding innovative Indian farmers.

What is needed now for transforming Indian farm sector in the WTO regime is the new strategy to increase income of the farmers. Indian farmers with small size of land are a great potential market if their incomes are increased substantially through market reforms and remunerative prices for their agriculture produce. Agriculture policy vintage of the 1970s has become now outmoded and bold policy of farmers' income at the center stage of development is essential. It is this aspect which has been highlighted and stressed in this book. The farmers will have to be more active to get implemented strategies and programs enunciated in the foregoing Chapters.

Epilogue

Farmers' Action for Income Revolution (FAIR)

The analysis in the foregoing Chapters focuses sharply on the income of the farmers as the target that should be pursued. Mere targeting of increase in food grains production and productivity is no guarantee that income of the farmers will increase ipso facto. The beginning of civilization depended on agriculture so does its future. It can not be sustained if farmers do not get grains but only the chaff. In spite of small size of land, the majority of the farmers will have to be provided with the reasonable standard of living. Accelerated increase in rural infrastructure activities have to compensate for the small size of the farms. It means more supplementary employment opportunity to farmer and his family. The land cultivation activity by the farmers is an income sharing arrangement with the land less labour which he employs. The cost of hired labour in the total cost of cultivation is about one third. If farmer's income increases it will further percolate in the rural economy and its multiplier effect will give rise to more productive economic activities. The experience of the farmers during the last 50 years with many government programs is that these programs have not significantly helped in increasing his income on a sustained basis and much less during the last five years.

The reason for this is the rate of growth of the agricultural economy moving at a snails pace. If agricultural sector of the economy is taken as separate entity of Indian economy's growth performance, then Indian economy of over 700 million rural population is growing at the rate of 1.5 per cent to 2 per cent. Indian economy's over all growth rate of 7 to 8 per cent hinges mainly on growth of the Service sector and moderately on manufacturing sector. There is not much of reverse income flow from service and manufacturing to agriculture. In such a slow moving economy burdened with two third of India's population, how can the income of the farmers increase. For the majority of the farmers it is hand to mouth existence. It is in this context that Income Revolution for the farmers is needed urgently. Many institutional arrangements and reforms suggested in the foregoing Chapters point out to this revolution. The Commissions and Committees normally suggest and recommend about what should be done to increase production and productivity. But none have come forward with design for enhancing farmer's income on a sustained basis. What is required now is the action on the part of the farmers to stand united to ask for their share of income in the national cake. Hence the Farmers' Action for Income Revolution (FAIR) is advocated so that they increase their income on a sustained basis.

FAIR is an attempt to give blue print to farmers to unite themselves affiliated on the basis of size of land (marginal and small)' and commodities. Unless farmers unite themselves as food grains farmers or wheat/rice/oilseeds farmers and do demand–supply management and market their produce aggressively or in collaboration with end users, their income will not increase. The experience of the farmers in developed countries is a testimony to the fact that Farmers' own Councils or Boards have been the single most important factor that helped them in increasing their income. The Soyabean farmers of USA improved their lot by forming American Soyabean Association which made the farmers strong to get better return for their produce. Same was the case of Sonoma County farmers of California who collectively pursued marketing policies that helped them to increase income. Its time for the Indian farmers to stand united under Commodity Boards/ Council to chart out an income revolution policy for them and ask for government support and collaborate with the corporate sector on an equal footing. Besides this, they will have to demand more infrastructure investment in agriculture to change the landscape of the rural economy. In this connection part of the idle foreign exchange reserves can be used in creating Infrastructure Investment Fund for Farmers to finance building up physical and institutional infrastructure as detailed in the Chapters.

The most important area that needs to be tackled is to increase the size of farmers' land holding on a collective action. To bring together farmers with different sizes of land on voluntary partnership basis is going to be a critical factor in increasing income. Sub-optimal marginal and small farms can not be extended beyond a limit by use of irrigation, fertilizer and high yielding varieties. Hence the organizational efforts by the farmers themselves through Commodity Boards/ Councils will be extremely important. NGOs and Cooperatives with experience in organizing the farmers can help and government can provide financial and organizational assistance. In this case, the existing farmers' organizations with different socio-political colours can draw blue print to help the farmers in different areas to work collectively to draw up production and marketing programs. In developed countries like EU the income enhancement program for farmers was made an integral part of Common Agriculture Policy (CAP) through supply-demand management and marketing support. Such an arrangement will be in place only when farmers' organizations will take up the initiatives.

It is not enough to plan for the enhancement of increase in farmers' income. What is needed is to build up national and State level indicators of increase in farmers' income. Such an indexing of farmers' income would help in targeting the same in given time frame. Such Indexing has been explained in Chapter VI. Government will have to organize this work and bring out such indices every six months or annually for better monitoring. It is the farmers' organizations who can insist on such institutional arrangements. Hence the FAIR will be in the right direction for sustained increase in income.

Annexure

Annex I

State-wise Agri-GDP* and Rural Population 1991 and 2001

Agri-GDP(1993-94 prices) Rs. Lakhs

Population lakhs

State	*Agri-GDP*		*Population*		*Per Capita Agri-GDP*	
	1990-91	*2001-02*	*1990-91*	*2001-02*	*1990-91*	*2001-02*
A.P.	1955209	2754705	486.2	552.2	4021	4988
Arunachal	49622	33354	7.5	8.7	6616	3842
Assam	571256	728366	199.3	232.5	2866	3084
Bihar	1639945	1711073	578.2	741.9	2836	2317
Goa	25149	44761	69.0	68.0	3645	6582
Gujarat	1254068	1765402	270.6	316.9	4634	5539
Haryana	1054731	1403354	124.1	149.7	8499	9374
Himachal	184407	233315	47.2	54.8	3483	4257
J&K		378388		75.6		5005
Karnataka	1528970	2324010	310.7	348.1	4921	6676
Kerala	909241	1084562	214.2	235.7	4245	4517
Madhya Pradesh	2091072	1957715	508.4	442.8	4113	4421
Maharashtra	2321350	3240670	483.9	567.3	4797	5712
Manipur	40934	55048	13.3	18.2	3078	3024
Meghalaya	38064	63061	14.4	18.5	3635	3408
Mizoram	12978	28099	3.7	4.5	3507	6244
Nagaland	29947	96997	10.0	16.4	2995	5987
Orissa	866410	968801	274.1	312.1	3233	3101
Punjab	1570451	2062066	142.9	160.4	10989	12337
Rajasthan	1574317	2133413	339.4	432.7	4639	3652

Contd..

Contd..

State	Agri-GDP		Population		Per Capita Agri-GDP	
	1990-91	*2001-02*	*1990-91*	*2001-02*	*1990-91*	*2001-02*
Sikkim	16561	16211	3.1	4.8	5342	3377
Tamil Nadu	1333247	1790632	367.8	348.7	3627	5135
Tripura	63094	125127	23.4	26.5	2696	4728
U.P.	3833358	4792848	1115.1	1315.4	3438	3571
W.B.	1734396	2602238	493.7	577.3	3513	4508

Agri-GDP: Value of Output of Agriculture and Livestock.

Source: National Account Statistics: Central Statistical Organization, Govt. of India.

Population Census: Registrar General, Ministry of Home Affairs.

Agricultural Statistics At A Glance: Ministry of Agriculture.

Annex II

Return to Farmer Per Hectare at MSP/SMP 2003-04

Commodity	*Av. Yield Kg/hectare*	*MSP Rs./Qnt*	*Return per Hectare Rs.*	*MPCR* Rs.*
Rice	2051	550	11,280	188
Wheat	2707	630	17,016	284
Jawar	772	505	3,897	64
Bajra	1134	505	5,726	95
Maize	1983	505	10,014	167
Arhar	690	1360	9,384	156
Moong	302	1370	4,137	97
Urad	423	1370	5,795	116
Ground Nut	1384	1400	19,376	323
Rapeseed	1152	1155	13,306	222
Soyabean	1208	840	10,147	169
Sunflower	539	1250	6,737	122
Jute	1923	860	16,538	276
Cotton	307	1725/1925	5,296/5910	82/99
Sugarcane	59,119	73	43,157	719

*Monthly Per Capita Return of Farmer Household of 5 members.

Source: CACP Report for the crops sown during 2004-05 Season.

Annex III

MSP Recommended by State Governments for Kharif Crops of 2004-05

Rs. Quintal

	Paddy Common	*Jowar*	*Bajra*	*Maize*	*Tur*	*Moong*	*Urd*
CACP's MSP	560	505	505	505	1360	1370	1370
States							
A.P.	645	800	706	538	1784	1700	1859
Chattisgarh	610	530	530	530	1410	1420	1420
Gujrat	800	710	615	625	1880	1740	1800
Haryana	680		625	625			
Himachal	550	505	505	505	1360	1370	1370
Karnataka	788	838	695	551	1728	1678	1673
M.P.	725	600	600		1450	1450	1450
Maharashtra	725	600	600	600	1450	1450	1450
Orissa	600		600		1510	1570	1550
Punjab	655		792		1768	1781	1820
Rajasthan		530	530	530	1450	1450	1450
UP	590						

Contd...

	Ground-nut	*Sesa-mum*	*Soyabean*	*Sun-flower*	*Cotton*	
					Medium	*Long*
CACP's MSP	1400		840/930	1250	1725	1925
A.P.	2268	2035			2700	2487
Chhatisgarh	1450	1535	890/980	1300	2400	2600
Gujarat	1800	2075			1830	2790
Haryana						2500
Himachal	1400	1485	840/930	1250	1725	1925
Karnataka	1903	2013	1187	1811		2097
M.P.	1525	1575	975/1125	1500	2200	2400
Maharashtra	2075		1420		2910	2781
Orissa	1620	2110			1800	2100
Punjab	1820					3128
Rajasthan	1450	1520	960			
U.P.			1300			

Source: CACP report for the crop sown during 2004-05 season.

Annex IV

Marketed Surplus Ratio (MSR) of Important Agricultural Commodities (All India Weighted Average) per cent

Commodity	*1999-2000*	*2001-02*
Rice	61.7	73.6
Wheat	56.5	73.3
Maize	67.3	66.0
Jawar	47.6	59.5
Bajra	61.7	56.9
Ragi	26.5	34.1
Arhar	63.5	77.2
Gram	71.8	81.2
Urad	90.5	85.5
Moong	74.4	74.7
Groundnut	62.2	80.1
Rapeseed & mustard	73.3	76.5
Soyabean	92.5	96.0
Sunflower	99.2	96.0
Sesasum	86.1	88.4
Saflower	89.2	81.4
Sugarcane	100.0	100.0
Cotton	83.8	86.9
Jute	97.5	93.2
Potato	47.8	91.1
Onion	98.5	100.0

Source: Agricultural Statistics At A Glance 2004. Ministry of Agriculture & Coop., Govt. of India.

Annex V

Commodity-Farmer Centric Income Kit

Food grains

Rice

No. of Farmers (No. of Holdings): 55.72 million. Area Cultivated: 45.82 million hectare. Marginal farmers: 36.2 million and Area cultivated: 13.2 million hectare. Small farmers: 10.1 million and Area: 10.5 million hectare. **Supply-Demand Balance:** Supply is adequate to meet present demand. Consumption is estimated to be 82.78 million tonnes against supply of 80.29 mt in 2004-05. Open market price (WPI) of rice decreased from 2000-01 to 2002-03 compared to 1999-2000 and WPI for 2003-4, though increased in 2002-03, was still lower than 1999-2000.

Price

MSP based income per hectare on the basis of average yield (20.5 quintals) per hectare works out to Rs.11,275 p.a. in 2003-04. If the yield is half the average yield per hectare the income will be just Rs.5637 p.a. for a marginal farmer. It is hardly sufficient for a family of 4/5 persons if there is no other source of income.

Non-Price Support

Procurement at MSP to be ensured at least where ever open market price falls below the MSP. Diversify Punjab and Haryana farmers from rice-wheat rotation to other crops to avoid water scarcity. Rice production in other States be encouraged. Full payment to farmers for purchase of rice by public agencies. This problem is serious in Vidarbha in Maharashtra and other places. MSP to incorporate increase in productivity by farmers by a suitable formula. Rice Farmers' Board to formulate production plan based on consumption trends to avoid surplus production. State governments and Central government to assist farmers in setting such Boards and provide initial funds. All farmers to contribute ½ per cent of 1 per cent of delivered price for raising funds for the Board for strengthening market demand, improving productivity and increasing profitability. Dedicated procurement of rice at MSP in central and eastern region to protect farmers' income there. Tie up between farmers and rice mills for lifting supplies from farm gates at least at the MSP.

Wheat

No. of farmers: 30.42 million. Area: 25.16 million hectare. Marginal farmers: 17.6 million and area cultivated: 5.7 million hectare. Small farmers: 5.6 million and area: 4.4 million. **Supply-Demand balance:** Maximum supply perceived by the market in 2004-05 at 75.85 million tonnes against consumption demand of 56.14 mt. During the last few years there has been excess supply of wheat in relation to current demand. WPI of wheat was lower in 2001-02 and 2002-03 compared to 1999-2000 and picked up recently.

Price

MSP based income per hectare on the basis of average yield (27 quintals) per hectare works out to Rs. 17,010 in 2003-04. If the yield is half the average, the income works out to just Rs. 8505 p.a. for a marginal farmer. If there is no other source of income, the income is hardly sufficient for livelihood of farmer's family.

Non-Price Support

Same as in case of rice farmers. Special procurement drive should be made for wheat farmers of central and eastern region to ensure income protection when open market prices fall below MSP. Similar Board of wheat farmers on the lines of Rice Board is needed to take number of non-price support measures for supply demand balance and conscious efforts to diversify to other crops where the production is more than the demand. This is especially needed in Punjab where problem of water scarcity and land degradation has arisen. Other potential wheat farmers need to be given incentives. Export of wheat needed to be developed on a more sustained basis by increasing quality and creating India Brand Wheat and wheat products.

Coarse Grains

No. of farmers: 35.54 million. Area: 31 million hectare. **Jowar** Marginal farmers: 3.9 million and area cultivated: 1.4 million hectare. Small farmers: 3.4 million and area: 2.6 million hectare. **Bajra** marginal farmers: 2.6 million and area cultivated: 1 million hectare. Small farmers: 1.8 million and area: 1.6 million hectare. **Supply-Demand balance:** Supply in excess of demand. The consumption demand is declining as coarse grains have become inferior in the consumption pattern of urban people. The production and consumption is highly localized. Chronic demand deficiency is the main problem. Even there is no evidence that demand of coarse grains is rising as animal feed. The coarse grains have short shelf life and storage becomes difficult.

Price

MSP based income per hectare works out to be low. For 2003-04, for Jowar farmers it is Rs.3898 p.a. and for maize farmers Rs. 10,000/–Even at average yield, for one hectare farmers income is extremely low to sustain his family and especially when open market prices are lower than the MSP and very meagre procurement support. The production depends on vagaries of monsoon making the farmers extremely miserable.

Non-Price Support

Some compensatory payments in cash are needed to divert these farmers to some other remunerative crops. Given the climatic conditions it may not be feasible beyond a point. Alternatively, concerted efforts are required to generate more demand by processing these grains as health food. The fibre content and easy digestibility are favourable factors. 35.5 million coarse grains farmers will have to set up their own Council or Board to get assured relief through dedicated procurement by public and private agencies and adjusting supply to demand for coarse grains. Except for small quantity of maize exports there is no export of other coarse grains. The acceptable animal feed can be developed to increase demand for coarse grains.

This institutional arrangement in the initial stages will have to be prompted by the government, NGOs and professional marketing agencies.

It is not as if there is no production of coarse grains in the world. According to FAO, in 2003-04 the global production was of the order of 931 million tonnes. Of this half is accounted for by USA, Canada, Argentina and Australia. Exports are to the tune of 105 million tonnes. If 35.5 million coarse farmers are united and given support to generate domestic and export demand, size of their income can be increased. Non-price support is the key to increase income of coarse grain farmers. They can not be left high and dry because of demand deficiency. If Soyabean can be diversified in to different uses as shown in the Box in Chapter 4, why similar innovative schemes can not be operated for these farmers. Non-price support is crucial for coarse grain farmers to increase the size of their income kit.

Pulses

No. of farmers: 15.17 million. Area under cultivation: 9.18 million hectare. **Arhar:** Marginal Farmers: 2.55 million. Area cultivated: 45 lakh hectares. Small farmers: 2.27 million. Area: 69 lakh hectares. Gram: Marginal farmers: 2.22 million. Area cultivated: 58 lakh hccatre. Small farmers: 1.58 million. Area: 85 lakh hectare. **Supply-Demand balance:** Production shows a declining trend as area under cultivation has decreased at the rate of 0.79 per cent. The gap between demand and supply of pulses has widened leading to increase in imports. Current Household Demand 12.23 million tonnes + Non-HH demand greater than the supplies of 14.28 MT. In 2003-04 higher prices encourage imports that dampen prices affecting farmer's income adversely.

Price

Large imports make it difficult to maintain MSP and safeguarding farmers' interests. Price of Urad in 2003 below MSP and for Moong in Jan. 2004. Prices of Urad in international market also ruled below MSP. Market intervention by NAFED fell short of the required quantity. Large imports further dampened the prices.

Non-Price Support

Production and productivity to be increased with adequate price support of MSP with intervention purchases (NAFED) where the open market prices fall below MSP. Current import duty (1-3-04) is 10 per cent while the Bond duty is 100 per cent. Scope for rationalization of import duty so that landed prices of pulses remain above the MSP and thereby incentive to farmers to increase production and earn higher income. Balance sheet of pulses demand and supply needs to be prepared and Farmers' Pulses Board can take lead.

Oilseeds: No. of farmers: 20.26 million. Area cultivated 17.27 million hectare.

Supply-Demand Balance

Production: 24.98 million tonnes in 2003-04. Imports 30 per cent of domestic production. Supply less than demand.

Price

Open market prices higher than MSP. For diversification of crops to oilseeds MSP increased substantially by Rs.30 to Rs.35 per quintal. International prices also prevail high. Imports are about 3 to 4 million tonnes.

Non-Price Support

Area under oilseeds to be increased by reducing emphasis on production of wheat and rice. Irrigation coverage of oilseeds is to increase and better lands brought under the cultivation of oilseeds. Increased production and yield will increase farmers' income when prices are rising. Soyabean production can be accelerated as has been done by the American Soyabean Association. Bio-diesel is produced from Soyabean in USA and mixed (20 per cent) with petroleum as also used in the production of ink and paints. Similar efforts may be encouraged for Soya farmers to increase their income. Similarly there is good export demand for Nigerseed produced by tribals of Orissa, M.P. and Chhatisgarh and Maharashtra. Unit value of exports is higher than the MSP and there is great scope to increase production and increase the income of tribal farmers. Oilseeds Farmers' Organization can be formed to coordinate with oil mills on a sustained basis to benefit mutually. Current import duty of 30 per cent on oilseeds can be rationalized with reference to Bond duty of 100 per cent for the benefit of the farmers.

Cotton

No. of farmers: 6.78 million. Area cultivated: 9.47 million hectare. Marginal Farmers: 1.55 million. Area: 0.73 mh. Small farmers: 1.95 million. Area: 1.82 mh.

Supply-Demand Balance

Supply (Production + Stock) 2004-05: 201 lakh bales (production 167.50 lakh bales + Stock 24.50 lakh bales). Demand (Mill and non-mill): 176 lakh bales. Supplies higher than demand resulting in fall in cotton prices. World cotton supply of 31.8 million tonnes higher than demand of 21.18 million tonnes.

Price

Over all cotton prices in the domestic and international market are depressed. With the arrival of cotton in the domestic market in November-December, the prices sometime fall below MSP. States announce higher cotton prices which they can not sustain. The farmers are not paid the price in full and farmer's payment is held up. MSP based income per hectare for 2003-04 works out to Rs. 5296 (Av. Yield 3.07 quintal x Rs.1725 for F414) to Rs. 5910 Av. Yield × Rs. 1925 for H-4). If the average yield is less or size of land is less than one hectare or open market price is less than MSP and no purchase at MSP, the income of the farmer decreases.

Non-Price Support

Due to unfavourable price trend of cotton, farmers are switching to other crops. However, to keep up the production level to meet future demand, more incentives to increase yield need to be given. Assured purchase at MSP by Cotton Corporation of India (CCI) is needed if the prices fall below MSP. Scheme of Monopoly Purchase of Cotton of Maharashtra government has become unsustainable with the surplus production of cotton. State announced prices create distortion in the market and being unsustainable due to limitations of State finances, they need to be discontinued in the interest of farmers. The use of genetically modified cotton seeds should be provided to farmers at affordable rates for increasing the yield.

MSPs fixed by CACP are mainly for traditional varieties of cotton. New varieties of cotton are now grown and MSP for such varieties should be fixed at the earliest to ensure proper returns to farmers. Cotton Corporation of India can be upgraded to promotional agency for better dialogue with farmers and monitor incomes of the farmers. Cotton thread machines are now available in the market. They can be introduced in the market for purchase of cotton on the basis of the length of the cotton for on-the-spot payment. This can be started on a pilot scale and adopted as a universal scheme for payment to farmers. Export market for Indian cotton should be expanded and India Brand Cotton is to be marketed on the pattern of US Cotton. Indian cotton is not inferior but needs marketing support. If USA can sell its cotton to China at high transport cost why India can not sell its cotton to China when it has transport cost advantage. Cotton farmers will have to be more active by forming Indian Cotton Farmers' Board (ICFB) to deal with price and non-price support to increase their income. ICFB's partnership with textiles mills can be mutually beneficial and intermediaries can be avoided that will reduce transaction cost of the farmers. Other organizational arrangements have been given in Chapter on Agriculture Marketing.

Sugarcane

No. of farmers: 6.59 million. Area cultivated: 3.92 million hectare. Marginal farmers: 3.1 million and Area: 1.6 mh. Small farmers: 0.88 million and Area: 0.98 mh.

Supply-Demand Balance

Production 279 million tonnes in 2002-03. Sugar cane can not be stocked as its quality deteriorates. About 60 per cent used for sugar production, 30 per cent for gur and khandsari and remaining for seed, feed and chewing. Sugar mills are the captive consumers of sugarcane.

Price : SMP

Under the Sugarcane Act the Statutory Minimum Price is fixed at 8.5 per cent recovery and this has to be paid by the sugar mills and others. There is no open market price of sugar as such though State governments announce their own price for sugarcane. The State announced prices are found to be aligned with the actual price paid by the sugar mills in the previous season. Some times these prices create distortion in sugarcane supply to sugar mills. The sugar cane farmers are initially paid SMP and at the end of the sugar season, based on the actual recovery, the revenue is shared with farmers under agreed formula. SMP based income of the farmer at average yield per hectare works out to Rs.49,786 (682 quintals av. Yield × SMP Rs.73 per quintal) for 2003-04. Farmer's income decreases if the yield is below average or size of land is less than one hectare or he is not paid SMP or payment is held up. There is difference in the cost of cultivation in different zones. There is need that MSPs are to be fixed zone-wise to benefit the farmers in particular zone.

Non-Price Support

The income of the cane farmer depends upon the profitability of sugar mills. With the full deregulation of sugar mills (levy sugar now only 10 per cent) and bumper production and stocks of sugar amounting to 29.5 million tonnes against the demand of 19 million tonnes, the price of sugar started falling from 1999-2000 till 2003-04 and is still not showing any significant upward trend. This resulted in low profits for sugar mills. Though the mills are supposed to pay the farmers as per the Act, they are not paid in full. The arrears are to the tune of Rs.3500 cro. The world production of sugar is also in excess of consumption and there is fall in the world price of sugar as well.

Outlet for excess stock of sugar of 6 million tonnes (stock 10 mt minus 4 mt minimum required) needs to be found out through exports. India should enter into the quota market for sugar on a regular basis to dispose of excess production. Russia is good export market. Russia imports of 3.65 million tonnes of sugar at nominal tariff of 5 per cent under the quota and this market can be explored. Raw and refined sugar production for export needs to be dedicated to earn more profit by sugar mills.

Sugarcane Farmer's Organizations at the all India and State level need to be formed to safeguard farmers' income and better return on their yield. The initial payment may not be limited to SMP. It should be added further based on the last three years agreed formula payment. This will be an incentive to farmers to continue cultivation of sugarcane and increase the yield. Only marginal payment at the end of the season may be settled. All the recommendations made by various Committees of the government having a bearing on farmer's income need to be implemented on priority and farmers' organization monitor and follow it up. CACP's recommendation that SMP be announced at least one year in advance to give the right price signal needs to be implemented urgently.

Rationalization of taxes and levies on sugarcane and sugar is also required that will support and add to farmer's income. Total revenue earned from the processing of sugar and by products such as alcohol and other products should be taken into account in giving the price of sugarcane to farmers. Ethanol produced from sugar is a commercially viable product. The technology has been developed by Brazil which is running its automobiles on ethanol. This is additional source of income and employment for sugarcane farmers. Steps can be taken by government to import this technology that will generate employment and income for sugarcane farmers. Sugarcane farmers' Organization can pursue this with the government.

Jute

No. of farmers: 49 lakh. Area cultivated: 1.39 lakh.

Supply-Demand Balance

2003-04: Total Supply: 131 lakh bales (Production 90 lakh bales + 7 lakh bales import +34 lakh bales opening stock). Total demand 101 lakh bales. Closing stock of 30 lakh bales has adverse impact on price level unless procurement is done by Jute Corporation of India.

Price

MSP base income for 2003-04 works out to Rs. 9997 per hectare (Av. Yield 11.59 quintals per hectare x MSP Rs. 860 per quintal).

Non-Price Support

MSP, as mentioned for other commodities, should be announced before commencement of the sowing season so that farmer gets appropriate price signal. In addition, dedicated procurement operation is required to maintain the level of MSP. Buffer stock of about 5 lakh bales can be built in the coming years. 171 procurement centres of JCI are adequate and farmers in remote areas are not served. JCI needs to expand its network for procurement from remote areas and if required Service Cooperatives can be involved in this operation on a regular basis for the benefit of the farmers. There is already over production of jute vis-à-vis demand and duty free import from Bangladesh is further aggravating the difficulties of disposing of excess stocks. This duty free import needs to be stopped or discouraged by imposing import duty. Farmer-government partnership supported by the private sector should take up promotion of jute products to generate domestic and international demand. It has been identified that jute based geo-textile can be used in building as road construction material in rural areas.

The contents of the above Income Kit are applicable to farmers producing fruits and vegetables and other agriculture produce. The crucial stage in agriculture development has been reached where farmers have to unite themselves by forming Commodity Organizations to safeguard their income.

Annexure VI

AoA from Uruguay to Hong Kong

The objective of AoA is to establish fair and market oriented trading system and reform process is to be initiated as per Uruguay Round through the negotiation of commitments on support and protection. The long term objective is to provide substantial progressive reductions in agriculture support and protection over agreed period of time. Accordingly the following time table was laid down.

Market Access

Tariff (Base 1986-88)	*Developed Countries (1995-2000)*	*Developing Countries (1995-2004)*
Average Cut for all agri. products	– 36%	–15%
Minimum cut per product line	–24%	–10%

Domestic Support

Domestic Support Base (Base 1986-88)	*Developed Countries (1995-2000)*	*Developing Countries (1995-2004)*
Aggregate Measure of Support (AMS)	–20%	–13%

Export Subsidies

Export Subsidies (Base 1986-88)	*Developed Countries (1995-2000)*	*Developing Countries (1995-2004)*
Export value of Subsidies (outlays)	–36%	– 24%
Subsidized operations	–21%	–14%

The above time table was hardly adhered to by developed countries. The WTO conferences were opposed by anti-globalization organizations and there came up sharp differences on the timing and the quantum of reduction in subsidization of agriculture sector by developed countries.

The **Doha Conference** held on 13th November 2001 reiterated that reductions in domestic support and protection applies to all WTO Members. But developing countries including India argued that subsidies and protection are needed to ensure food security to support small scale farming, to make for lack of capital or prevent the rural poor migrating to already over-congested cities. These became an integral part of the mandated agricultural negotiation. There is a clear commitment to review the provisions of Special and Differential (S&D) treatment for developing countries.

As a follow up of Doha, Conference was held in **Cancun, Mexico,** on 31st August 2003 which also considered Singapore issues relating to investment, competition policy, transparency in government procurement and trade facilitations. EU and USA negotiated joint text Compromise Draft. The emphasis shifted from modalities of implementing to framework of negotiation. US and EU chose to work on "framework" of key issues rather than the modalities. The frame work draft had a number of gaps. US and EU deliberately avoided, including numbers, such as percentages and coefficients for tariff restrictions. They also left open the question of special treatment for developing countries saying that they ran out of time.

At this stage, 39 WTO Members have reserved the right to use a combined total of 6156 special safeguards on agriculture products, 43 WTO Members have combined total of 1425 tariff quotas in their commitment and 25 WTO Members have subsidy for exports for those products on which they have commitment to reduce the subsidies. At this rate how can the AoA be implemented ?

The World Bank Report released before the Cancun Conference also stated that the developed countries tariffs faced by developing countries exporters in agriculture is several times higher than in manufactures. This is resulting in denying the income generation of billions of dollars in developing countries.

The 20 developing countries including India – G20–circulated their own draft. So at the start of 2004, the favoured approach came to be to tackle framework first and then complete the modalities. Final deadline for negotiations is 1st January 2005.

Hong Kong Conference December 2005
DOHA WORK PROGRAMME

Draft Ministerial Declaration 18th December 2005

Agriculture Negotiations

On domestic support, there will be three bands for reductions in Final Bound Total AMS and in the overall cut in trade-distorting domestic support, with higher linear cuts in higher bands. In both cases, the Member with the highest level of permitted support will be in the top band, the two Members with the second and third highest levels of support will be in the middle band and all other Members, including all developing country Members, will be in the bottom band. In addition, developed country Members in the lower bands with high relative levels of Final Bound Total AMS will make an additional effort in AMS reduction. Developed countries to achieve effective cuts in trade-distorting domestic support consistent with the Framework. The overall reduction in trade-distorting domestic support will still need to be made even if the sum of the reductions in Final Bound Total AMS, *de minimis* and Blue Box payments would otherwise be less than that overall reduction. Developing country Members with no AMS commitments will be exempt from reductions in *de minimis* and the overall cut in trade-distorting domestic support. Green Box criteria will be reviewed in line with paragraph 16 of the Framework, *inter alia,* to ensure that programmes of developing country Members that cause not more than minimal trade-distortion are effectively covered.

The parallel elimination of all forms of export subsidies and disciplines on all export measures with equivalent effect to be completed by the end of 2013. This will be achieved in a progressive and parallel manner, to be specified in the modalities, so that a substantial part is realized by the end of the first half of the implementation period. Declaration notes emerging convergence on some elements of disciplines with respect to export credits, export credit guarantees or insurance programmes with repayment periods of 180 days and below. It was agreed that such programmes should be self-financing, reflecting market consistency, and that the period should be of a sufficiently short duration so as not to effectively circumvent real commercially-oriented discipline. As a means of ensuring that trade-distorting practices of STEs are eliminated, disciplines relating to exporting STEs will extend to the future use of monopoly powers so that such powers cannot be exercised in any way that would circumvent the direct disciplines on STEs on export subsidies, government financing and the underwriting of losses. On food aid, it is confirmed to maintain an adequate level and to take into account the interests of food aid recipient countries. To this end, a "safe box" for bona fide food aid will be provided to ensure that there is no unintended impediment to dealing with emergency situations. Beyond that, elimination of commercial displacement is ensured. To this end, effective disciplines on in-kind food aid, monetization and re-exports so that there can be no loop-hole for continuing export subsidization is agreed. The disciplines on export credits, export credit guarantees or insurance programmes, exporting state trading enterprises and food aid will be completed by 30 April 2006 as part of the modalities, including appropriate provision in favour of least-developed and net food-importing developing countries as provided for in paragraph 4 of the Marrakesh Decision. The date above for the elimination of all forms of export subsidies, together with the agreed progressivity and parallelism, will be confirmed only upon the completion of the modalities. Developing country Members will continue to benefit from the provisions of Article 9.4 of the Agreement on Agriculture for five years after the end-date for elimination of all forms of export subsidies.

On market access, the progress made on *ad valorem* equivalents was noted. Developing country Members will have the flexibility to self-designate an appropriate number of tariff lines as Special Products guided by indicators based on the criteria of food security, livelihood security and rural development. Developing country Members will also have the right to have recourse to a Special Safeguard Mechanism based on import quantity and price triggers, with precise arrangements to be further defined. Special Products and the Special Safeguard Mechanism shall be an integral part of the modalities and the outcome of negotiations in agriculture.

On other elements of special and differential treatment, we note in particular the consensus that exists in the Framework on several issues in all three pillars of domestic support, export competition and market access and that some progress has been made on other special and differential treatment issues.

It is agreed to intensify work on all outstanding issues to fulfil the Doha objectives, in particular, to establish modalities no later than 30 April 2006 and to submit comprehensive draft Schedules based on these modalities no later than 31 July 2006.

Cotton

— All forms of export subsidies for cotton will be eliminated by developed countries in 2006.

— On market access, developed countries will give duty and quota free access for cotton exports from least-developed countries (LDCs) from the commencement of the implementation period.

— [It is recognized that the objective is that, as an outcome for the negotiations, trade distorting domestic subsidies for cotton production should be reduced more ambitiously than under whatever general formula is agreed and that it should be implemented over a shorter period of time than generally applicable.]

With regard to the development assistance aspects of cotton, we welcome the Consultative Framework process initiated by the Director-General to implement the decisions on these aspects pursuant to paragraph 1.b of the Decision adopted by the General Council on 1 August 2004. We take note of his Periodic Reports and the positive evolution of development assistance noted therein. Director-General is urged to further intensify his consultative efforts with bilateral donors and with multilateral and regional institutions, with emphasis on improved coherence, coordination and enhanced implementation and to explore the possibility of establishing through such institutions a mechanism to deal with income declines in the cotton sector. Noting the importance of achieving enhanced efficiency and competitiveness in the cotton producing process, the development community is urged to further scale up its cotton-specific assistance and to support the efforts of the Director-General. In this context, Members are to promote and support South-South cooperation, including transfer of technology. The domestic reform efforts by African cotton producers aimed at enhancing productivity and efficiency are welcome, and are encouraged to deepen this process. The complementarity of the trade policy and development assistance aspects of cotton is affirmed. The Director-General is to set up an appropriate follow-up and monitoring mechanism.

Annexure VII

Organic Farming in EU Countries

The use of chemical became more prevalent in EU countries during and after second World War to increase food grains production across Europe quickly. But in 1960s, 70s and 80s farmers and consumers started showing concern about detrimental environmental impact of intensive farming. Farmers started showing interest as prices for conventionally produced commodities fell. U.K published organic standards in 1967 and common standards introduced across EU in 1992. Community logo was introduced and adopted by EC for organic production in May 2001. The Copenhagen Declaration introduced European Action Plan for the development of organic farming and national support program in the whole of Europe. U.K has nine bodies for certification of organic farming. Denmark was the first to adopt a law of organic farming and national support program. FAO Committee on Agriculture adopted in 1999 a Report on organic agriculture study of 18 European countries. Organic farming favours higher employment as it requires more labour.

Support is provided for organic farming. Organic Aid Schemes are in operation since 1994. EU has Rural Development Regulation which provides compensation for income lost during conversion period. Conversion period for annual crops is two years and three years for perennial crops. Annual payments are made per hectare of land converted for the first five years following conversion. The whole farm is not required to be converted to organic farm. It can be converted into batches. The scheme was reviewed in 1998 and payment increased from 1999 to reflect cost of conversion, 50 per cent is funded by the Members and 50 per cent by EC. Organic Farming Research Unit provides advice to farmers. Organic Food Markets are being developed and encouraged. So far 15 EU members have converted 3.34 million acres to organic farming and targets have been set up for conversion in future. EU is silently going ahead with organic farming to replace chemical farming.

Bibliography

1. State of Indian Farmers: A Millennium Study. Ministry of Agriculture and Coop.
2. Cost of Cultivation and Farm Income: Prof. Abhijit Sen
3. Agriculture Statistics At A Glance 2005: Ministry of Agriculture and Coop.
4. Economic Survey 2004-05: Ministry of Finance.
5. Agriculture Exports: Prof. B.B. Bhatacharya.
6. Globalisation and Liberalization of Agriculture: G S Bhalla
7. NSSO 59th Round i. Situation Assessment Survey of Farmers ii. Household Consumption Expenditure of Farmers iii. Debt and Investment: Deptt. Of Statistics, Ministry of Planning and Program implementation.
8. Institutions and Economic Policies for Pro-poor Agriculture Growth: DFID, Social Science Research Unit, Project 7989. Millennium Study on Indian Farmers–An Overview: Dr Y K Alagh.
10. Special and Differential Treatment for Developing Countries in Agreement on Agriculture: Non-Paper by Ministry of Commerce.
11. FAO Guide (2001) "Contract Farming: Partnership for Growth".
12. Report of the Commission for Agriculture Costs and Prices 2005-06: Ministry of Agriculture and Coop.

13. Technology Generation and IPR Issues: Ghayar Khan.
14. India: Agri-Business and Commercial Agriculture Assessment (TA 4192-IND) Final Report: Asian Development Bank, Manila, Philippines.
15. IPR and Agricultural Interest of Developing Countries: Jayashree Watal.
16. Food Processing Policy 2005: Ministry of Food Processing.
17. Abhijit Sen Committee Report: Ministry of Food and Consumer Affairs.
18. Report of Task Force on Revival of Cooperative Credit Institutions (30th December 2004): Prof. Vaidyanathan Committee: Reserve Bank of India.
19. Prof. Vyas Committee on Flow of Rural Credit: Reserve Bank of India.
20. Indian Cotton Manual 2002-03: East India Cotton Association.
21. Cotton Market setting, Trade Policies and Issues: John Baffes.: World Bank Policy Research Working Paper 3218, Feb. 2004.
22. Improving Income of Farmers and Rural People: Lasak Klank
23. EU Commission Agriculture Policy: Interim Report: Inter American Development Bank Report. First Draft. Sept. 17, 2002.
24. Census of India 2001: Registrar General of India, Ministry of Home Affairs.
25. National Accounts Statistics: Central Statistical Organization.
26. OECD Review of Agriculture Policies–China: OECD, Paris.
27. Starting a County Agriculture Marketing Reform: Paul Vasson. Lournal of Extension. Fall 1992. Vol.30. No.3
28. Soyabean: Year-in Review 2004: American Soyabean Association.
29. The Development of Post Harvest Systems and Agro-Industry as Strategy to Raise Income of the Rural Poor: International Food Policy Research Institute (IFPRI), Washington.
30. Family Farm in a Globalizing World: Michael Lipton. June 2005. IFPRI, Washington.

31. Common Agriculture Policy (CAP)of EU: European Commission.

32. European Union Policy–Common Agriculture Policy: Economic Research Service, US Deptt. Of Agriculture.

33. Agriculture Export Earnings: FAO Corporate Documents Repository.

34. Organic Europe: Bio Europe 2004: Organic Directory of Europe.

35. Reserve Bank of India Bulletins and Annual Reports.

36. Farming Systems and Poverty–Improving Farmers' livelihood in a changing world: John Dixon and Aidan Gulliver with David Gibson. Principal Editor: Malcom Half. FAO AND World Bank. 2001.

Index

P